PEACE IN THE STORM

"Perfect Peace in the Midst of Life's Scariest Storms"

JULIA WRIGHT FORTENBERRY

Full Circle Publishing
Biloxi, MS

Full Circle Publishing
PO Box 8549
Biloxi, MS 39535

For information address Full Circle Publishing Rights Department, PO Box 8549, Biloxi, MS 39535

First Paperback edition April 2017

Editing by Full Circle Publishing & Julie Keene

Cover Design/Graphics Illustrator by Jennifer Fortenberry Browder

Manufactured in the United States of America

ISBN-13: 978-0692872086 (Full Circle Publishing)
ISBN-10: 0692872086
BISAC: Religion / Christian Life / Spiritual Growth

TABLE OF CONTENTS

DEDICATION

This book can only be dedicated to my Savior, Jesus Christ and to my teacher, the Holy Spirit. Without Jesus Christ saving me, I would have nothing good in me to write about. Without the teaching of the Holy Spirit, far beyond religious doctrine, I never would have understood TRUTH. Jesus my Savior died as a sacrifice for my sins and brings His righteousness as a covering for me daily, showering me with His mercy, fresh and new every morning. The Holy Spirit nudges me and opens my eyes and opens my ears to hear Him teaching me the absolute TRUTH about our Holy Jehovah God. I am completely unworthy but by His precious gift to me Jesus makes me worthy to receive His mercy and His teachings. You too can have that same forgiveness and newness of life, just keep reading.

CHAPTER ONE

Wrestling With Trials and Tribulations

What kind of peace do you long for in your innermost being? Peace for the world from wars that rage and that put our service men and women in the grip of death and anguish? Peace in our schools and business from all the violence that we hear about almost daily? Peace in our streets and communities from the hard lines of divisive protests? Peace in your home from anger, bitterness, drugs, alcohol, abuse, unfaithfulness, financial distress, disharmony? OR peace in your heart and soul that can withstand any of these fears and circumstances?

Lord, Jesus Christ, please open the heart, soul and mind of the person reading this study. Please allow Your words to penetrate and speak deeply in her heart. Let Your Word be set in her mind so that there is permanent change in her from the inside out. You are our peace and our truth. To You, Heavenly Father, is due all the glory and honor that we may find as we study Your Word.

Let's look at the Hebrew and Greek words for peace. In Hebrew it is *shalom. Shalom*, as defined in the Holman Illustrated Bible Dictionary (2003, Holman Bible Publishers), means a condition or sense of harmony, well-being, prosperity. In Greek, it is *Eirene* which means the absence of hostility, strife or disorder; condition and sense of being safe and secure. Our typical greeting in America, or at least in the South, is "How are you?" But in Hebrew it would be "Shalom" which would be wishing someone to have peace. Wouldn't it be great if we greeted everyone with "Do you have peace today?" What an opening that would be to witness and minister to those around us! Sorry, I got off track for a moment. Back to our word – peace. The condition or sense of harmony and well-being, being safe and secure or the absence of hostility, strife and disorder. Is this what you are looking for in your life? Would you like a sense of harmony in all that you do? In your family life? In your work place? In your relationships with friends and loved ones? Do you want that feeling of well-being – to know that you are being provided with care in the deepest sense of the word? Do you want to know that not only today but that tomorrow you can be safe and secure no matter what the media tells you and no matter what your bank account shows and no matter what your weak and seemingly defeated body tells you? If this is what you long for in your life, then hang on through this study. We will look deeply into the truths of God's Word so that we can plant it in our hearts and hold onto it during times of trials and tribulations.

Well, that is a good place to start – looking at trials and tribulations. But wait you say, this is a study about peace. I don't want to learn about trials and tribulations. I have enough on-the-job experience with those. Well, this is where you must hold on tight to the Word. We must fully understand what the Word teaches us about the trials and tribulations that we face for us to fully understand the perfected peace that Jesus offers to us through His life, death and resurrection. We must battle the message of lies being put out through false prophets that if you just put on a happy face and claim the blessings that are out there for you, then you'll be happy, happy, happy all the time. That is not biblical and when you stand beside a loved one who is battling the agonizing daily pain of cancer or you stand beside a grave of a child or spouse and your heart is breaking, you cannot just put on a happy face. Yet, even in that circumstance, you can find the peace of God that surpasses all comprehension. There is a huge difference in the lies of the world about happiness and the unshakeable peace of God. Dear brothers and sisters in Christ, hold on and allow God to grow you in your understanding of His peace through the teaching of His Word.

Matthew 10:33-39,"But whoever denies Me before men, I will also deny him before My Father who is in heaven. Do not think that I came to bring peace on the earth; I did not come to bring peace, but a sword. For I came to SET A MAN AGAINST HIS FATHER, AND A DAUGHTER AGAINST HER MOTHER, AND A DAUGHTER-IN-LAW AGAINST HER MOTHER-IN-LAW; and A MAN'S ENEMIES WILL BE THE MEMBERS OF HIS HOUSEHOLD. He who loves father or mother more than Me is not worthy of Me; and he who loves son or daughter more than Me is not worthy of Me. And he who does not take his cross and follow after Me is not worthy of Me. He who has found his life will lose it, and he who has lost his life for My sake will find it."

Jesus wanted to clearly state to His followers that He did NOT come to the earth to establish some euphoric paradise where everyone was at perfect peace and happiness. He made it crystal clear, that to follow Him, there would be trials and tribulation and you would have to take up your cross which was a symbol of pain and suffering. So, use this passage to set in your mind the idea that just because you have Jesus does NOT in any way mean that you will have a life free of trials and tribulations. Also, as you look at the strong words of Jesus here, remember that we must take the whole counsel of the WORD and not form our beliefs around just one isolated verse. In Acts 20:27, Paul states that he did not shrink away from declaring the whole purpose (counsel) of God. We must understand that in choosing Christ to be our Savior and LORD, tribulations will come just as Christ Himself said but we also have the assurance that Jesus Christ overcame the trials and tribulations of this world and we are more than conquerors in HIM.

James 1:2-4, "A Consider it all joy, my brethren, when you encounter various trials, knowing that the testing of your faith produces endurance. And let endurance have its perfect result, so that you may be perfect and complete, lacking in nothing."

James 1:12-13, "A Blessed is a man who perseveres under trial; for once he has been approved, he will receive the crown of life which the Lord has promised to those who love Him."

Not only did Jesus say that we were going to have tribulations but that we are to count them as joy because of the faith that it produces in us. There are three times in my life that I have vivid memories of the peace of God that is beyond my comprehension that allowed me to count my trails as joy. The first is when we were trying to have a second child and we had gone through every medical procedure possible at that time and the doctor told me that not only was I not going to have a baby but that I must have a hysterectomy. This wise doctor who listened to our Heavenly Father through his practice, told me that he would give me a year to deal with my emotions before he would do the surgery. As I poured out my heart to God that year, I just knew He would give me the miracle that I so desperately wanted. Each week, I would linger on my knees asking God for a miracle. I would remind Him, as I lay across the floor of our prayer room at church, that He was a miracle-working God. Each month I would convince myself that He was lingering for dramatic effect. I even convinced myself for a while that I would go to the hospital for the surgery and they would discover that I was pregnant just minutes before they were to do surgery. At that time, I was teaching in public school and there was one child who stole my heart and he was not wanted by his mother nor his grandmother. He was being raised by his great-grandmother who was very frail and sick. I cried out to God, reminding Him that Gary and I would never allow that to happen to our child. We would be good parents and we would give our child a good home. However, as the day drew near for the surgery, I had to face that I might not get my miracle. The surgery would make it final. My hopes and dreams of a second child would be completely and utterly annihilated. Many family and friends had prayed with me and watched me agonize over this for a year. They began to ask what they should pray at that time. I simply ask them to pray for peace. When we arrived at the hospital the morning of surgery and were checking in, the receptionist looked at me almost with horror as she assigned the room that I was to go to. She looked at Gary and simply said, "I'm sorry." Well I surely began to wonder what was wrong with that room. It wasn't the room itself, but the location of the room. As we got off the elevator, we turned and there was the nursery and all the proud family members looking in awe and wonder at the newborn babies. As I thought my heart would fall out of my chest, they walked us to the room which was just before a set of locked double doors. It was the psychiatric ward. I thought, how funny, they are going to walk me past the babies that I can't have and push me completely over the edge and roll me right on into the psychiatric ward and lock me up. But with God that wasn't the case at all. The next morning, after surgery, as I was becoming more aware of my surroundings, the nurse ask me if I was in any pain and did I need more pain medicine. I told her that I was not in pain. She informed me that it appears I was using the pain pump quite a bit. I told her that I had not touched the pain pump. We both looked at Gary. He confessed that every time I moaned in my sleep, he pushed the button to keep me from hurting. After he got a scolding from the nurse, she decided to take the pain pump off since I was not in that much pain. She reassured me that they could give me oral pain medicine at any time I needed it. Several hours later she came back and asked if I needed any medicine and I assured her that I was not in pain. Later that evening she said that I would have to get up and walk but I could have pain medicines to help with that task and again I told her that I didn't hurt. The next day they went through this same routine again and this time as I said the words, "I don't hurt" it was as if a lightning bolt hit me. I didn't hurt. I walked down the hall by the babies and I didn't hurt. I had conversations with my husband and family and I DID NOT hurt. My body didn't hurt. My heart didn't hurt either. God gave the peace that passes all understanding. If I had not felt the depth of pain during that year, I would never have truly understood that perfect peace. I count that trial as joy because I came to KNOW my God so much deeper and I persevered.

The second time in my life that I experienced this God-delivered, authentic peace was when my mother had heart surgery in 1997. She had a scheduled by-pass surgery. They came out of the operating room and told us that she did great and they were closing her up and she would be in recovery shortly. However, before they could get her chest completely stitched back together, her heart stopped and they had to reopen her quickly and get her heart started again which they did. She went to ICU for 2 days and then to a cardiac care room. She was in the room less than 12 hours and her heart stopped again. They rushed her back to ICU and her heart stopped two more times over the course of another 12 hours. Every time they got her heart started again but they had to put the respirator down her trachea in a rushed and rough manner to keep oxygen going in her lungs. During this time, we asked friends to come and pray with us. As we began to pray, I released her to God and asked Him to take her home and I would be OK with that, I just didn't want to see her suffer the way she suffered that day. She was scared and trembling and her eyes were wild as if she was begging me to make it all stop. That evening, a group of friends and relatives joined us in the waiting room and we were in the process of making a prayer circle when a man was escorted into the waiting room by a nurse. He was dirty and his clothes were torn and ragged. He looked as if he had been beaten up and dragged through the dirt. He was visibly shaken and distraught over whatever brought him there that night. Before we began to pray, our minister asked me if it was OK to include him in our prayers and I was more than willing to do so. We asked him if he wanted to join us and he explained that he and his wife had just been in a motorcycle accident and she was rushed into surgery and he didn't know if she would live or not. He was thankful that we asked him to join us in prayer as we prayed over my mother and his wife. I never saw him again after that time. The next morning early, the nurse came and asked me to go in and see my mom. As I entered her ICU cubicle, I saw her eyes that were clear and peaceful. Her hands were not shaking and she could motion and communicate with me with no fear. Later that day after they removed the respirator, she asked what had happened to her. I explained all the events and then, almost as an after-thought, I told her about the man in the waiting room and how he allowed us to pray with him. She simply said, "Well, that is why then". I was stumped at that answer and asked her to explain. She said that is why God allowed all those things to happen to her so that we would be gathered in the waiting room as an army of prayer warriors to pray with that man when he arrived. Boy oh boy was I moved to a deeper understanding of our Jehovah God and I consider it joy that I could experience that trail. I persevered.

By my 55th birthday, I would have thought that I had endured enough trials and tribulations to fully understand the mighty power and provision of our great Jehovah God, but he wanted to teach me and Gary far greater things than we had ever known. My 55th birthday was July 24, 2016. On July 27, 2016, after 25 ½ years, Gary was laid off from his job at a large hospital in a nearby city effective immediately, no notice, no discussion, his job was over. Our financial security was over. Our health insurance was over. Our life plans were immediately out of our control. They did give him a one-month severance package so we were going to be able to catch our breath, consider his options with employment and then make an informed, and prayed-over decision. At least that is how we planned it. That was not God's plans though. The Saturday after he was laid off on Wednesday, we received a call from the nursing home where his mother resided. She was in her final stages of her battle with Alzheimer's disease and she would not live long. We stopped what we were doing and spent the next two weeks by her side. The Lord took her home August 16, 2016. So, the next week we went through the process of burying her and taking care of her final business. Now, in September, Gary and I decided to do some remodeling before he began a new job and he worked diligently redoing our kitchen and my office and our bedroom. He was working toward the two other bedrooms and our bathroom. Again, this was not in God's plans for us to finish this project at least at that time. On October 10th, I came home from work and Gary said he had to talk to me about a small growth in his mouth that was bothering him. He realized we didn't have any insurance but he needed to have it checked out as it was becoming uncomfortable and painful. We had 60 days from the date of his official dismissal letter to pick up the hospital insurance so we decided that we would call and see if we could get it reinstated but we were three days too late and they wouldn't budge on that date. So, what do we do? We called an oral surgeon and told the receptionist that we would pay cash but he needed to be seen. The doctor did the biopsy and we heard those dreaded words, "it is cancer." We began being told that no surgeon nor oncologist would see him if he didn't have insurance. How on earth were we going to get insurance now that he had a cancer diagnosis??? Gary and I had to do something we had never done in all our 38 years of marriage – we had to pray for every need and seek total provision from God and God alone. We had a host of family and friends praying with us but we had to give up every ounce of control that we might have thought we had and learn to trust God for every single provision in our lives. The cancer battle is hard, oh so very hard. But as we learned day by day and sometimes, minute by minute to trust God for every need, we learned just how powerful His provisions are and that they far surpass anything we might have found on our own. We count it joy that we learned to walk hand in hand with our Savior through this journey. We count it joy for His provisions – His abundant provisions. We count it joy for His testimony to become alive in us. We have both persevered.

For each of these life-altering events, we can say that we count those trials as joy for we KNOW our Father much, much more than we would have known Him without the trials.

Romans 5:3-5, "And not only this, but we also exult in our tribulations, knowing that tribulation brings about perseverance; and perseverance, proven character; and proven character, hope; and hope does not disappoint, because the love of God has been *poured out within our hearts through the Holy Spirit who was given to us."*

Again, Jesus is telling us to exult in our tribulations, not because of the tribulation, but because of what it will teach us about Him and how it will help us to grow. But let's back up two verses and see what was said just prior to this statement. Verses 1-2, *"Therefore, having been justified by faith, we have peace with God through our Lord Jesus Christ, through whom also we have obtained our introduction by faith into this grace in which we stand; and we exult in hope of the glory of God."* We don't exult because of the tribulation but because of the hope we have in the glory of God.

Romans 12:12-13, *"rejoicing in hope, persevering in tribulation, devoted to prayer, contributing to the needs of the saints, practicing hospitality."*

This verse is in the middle of a list that shows how we should live in Christ. It is just one more verse that says we will have tribulation but that we can have hope in Christ Jesus when we persevere.

So many people are being led to believe by the mighty false prophets of today, through the lies of satan, that if you are a Christ-follower and are walking the right path with God, that you will be blessed and not have trials and tribulations. When something goes wrong in your life, then they believe it was because of your lack of faith or because of some hidden sin in your life. Well, if that were true, I would have serious problems with the following biblical account. Paul was chosen by God to serve Him as one of the very first missionaries. His past was horrible as he was a murderer of Christians, but Jesus came and touched Paul's life and forgave him and changed him. The majority of the New Testament was written by Paul. If anyone should have had a blessed life after he accepted Jesus as Lord and Savior it would have certainly been Paul. Let's look at his own summary of his life and see what his life for Christ looked like. It is a lengthy passage but please don't skip any part of it as it holds great information about trials and tribulations and what our response should be to them.

2 Corinthians 11:16-12:10, "Again I say, let no one think me foolish; but if you do, receive me even as foolish, so that I also may boast a little. What I am saying, I am not saying as the Lord would, but as in foolishness, in this confidence of boasting. Since many boast according to the flesh, I will boast also. For you, being so wise, tolerate the foolish gladly. For you tolerate it if anyone enslaves you, anyone devours you, anyone takes advantage of you, anyone exalts himself, anyone hits you in the face. To my shame I must say that we have been weak by comparison. But in whatever respect anyone else is bold — I speak in foolishness — I am just as bold myself. Are they Hebrews? So am I. Are they Israelites? So am I. Are they descendants of Abraham? So am I. Are they servants of Christ? — I speak as if insane — I more so; in far more labors, in far more imprisonments, beaten times without number, often in danger of death. Five times I received from the Jews thirty-nine lashes. Three times I was beaten with rods, once I was stoned, three times I was shipwrecked, a night and a day I have spent in the deep. I have been on frequent journeys, in dangers from rivers, dangers from robbers, dangers from my countrymen, dangers from the Gentiles, dangers in the city, dangers in the wilderness, dangers on the sea, dangers among false brethren; I have been in labor and hardship, through many sleepless nights, in hunger and thirst, often without food, in cold and exposure. Apart from such external things, there is the daily pressure on me of concern for all the churches. Who is weak without my being weak? Who is led into sin without my intense concern? If I have to boast, I will boast of what pertains to my weakness. The God and Father of the Lord Jesus, He who is blessed forever, knows that I am not lying. In Damascus the ethnarch under Aretas the king was guarding the city of the Damascenes in order to seize me, and I was let down in a basket through a window in the wall, and so escaped his hands. Boasting is necessary, though it is*

not profitable; but I will go on to visions and revelations of the Lord. I know a man in Christ who fourteen years ago — whether in the body I do not know, or out of the body I do not know, God knows — such a man was caught up to the third heaven. And I know how such a man — whether in the body or apart from the body I do not know, God knows — was caught up into Paradise and heard inexpressible words, which a man is not permitted to speak. On behalf of such a man I will boast; but on my own behalf I will not boast, except in regard to my weaknesses. For if I do wish to boast I will not be foolish, for I will be speaking the truth; but I refrain from this, so that no one will credit me with more than he sees in me or hears from me. Because of the surpassing greatness of the revelations, for this reason, to keep me from exalting myself, there was given me a thorn in the flesh, a messenger of Satan to torment me — to keep me from exalting myself! Concerning this I implored the Lord three times that it might leave me. And He has said to me, "My grace is sufficient for you, for power is perfected in weakness." Most gladly, therefore, I will rather boast about my weaknesses, so that the power of Christ may dwell in me. Therefore I am well content with weaknesses, with insults, with distresses, with persecutions, with difficulties, for Christ's sake; for when I am weak, then I am strong."

No one that I know personally, and I would dare say the vast majority of Americans, has experienced anything remotely close to what Paul endured and yet he was grateful for the trials as it showed the power of God through his weaknesses. Let us grab hold of this passage and see our tribulations as opportunities to know the peace and comfort of God more dearly and to show others the power of Almighty God. When we allow Him to be LORD, we give our lives over to Him to use in any way that He deems necessary to draw others into the kingdom and to draw us closer to Him. Trials and tribulations force us to draw nearer to the One who can provide peace and shelter and comfort and healing.

Deuteronomy 8:1-10, "All the commandments that I am commanding you today you shall be careful to do, that you may live and multiply, and go in and possess the land which the Lord swore to give to your forefathers. You shall remember all the way which the Lord your God has led you in the wilderness these forty years, that He might humble you, testing you, to know what was in your heart, whether you would keep His commandments or not. He humbled you and let you be hungry, and fed you with manna which you did not know, nor did your fathers know, that He might make you understand that man does not live by bread alone, but man lives by everything that proceeds out of the mouth of the Lord. Your clothing did not wear out on you, nor did your foot swell these forty years. Thus you are to know in your heart that the Lord your God was disciplining you just as a man disciplines his son. Therefore, you shall keep the commandments of the Lord your God, to walk in His ways and to fear Him. For the Lord your God is bringing you into a good land, a land of brooks of water, of fountains and springs, flowing forth in valleys and hills; a land of wheat and barley, of vines and fig trees and pomegranates, a land of olive oil and honey; a land where you will eat food without scarcity, in which you will not lack anything; a land whose stones are iron, and out of whose hills you can dig copper. When you have eaten and are satisfied, you shall bless the Lord your God for the good land which He has given you."

The Lord allowed the Israelite children to wander around in the wilderness because of their sins and their lack of faith. Along the way, as they wandered in the wilderness, He tested them through trials and tribulations to see if they were going to remain faithful to Him when things were hard. This testing was building their devotion to God and their character that would be needed later in their lives. Because of His great love for them, when they had given themselves, 100% to God, He led them into the Promised Land. He gave them a land that was full of everything they needed and an abundance of those things that would make them feel secure and satisfied. We must see that God did not remove them from the trials and tribulations but more importantly, He never left them during their time of wandering. In the big picture, our entire lives are spent wandering through this wilderness seemingly controlled by satan. We are strangers, aliens, in a sinful land; children of God living amid moral decay and celebration of evil. The promised land, in the big picture, is for us in heaven. We are promised to walk streets of gold, live in beautiful mansions, and sit at the feet of our Savior, worshipping with the angels. However, for the here and now, in the small picture of our lives, God takes us through the valleys full of trials and tribulations and then brings us out the other side and allows us to live in brief interludes of the small promised lands here on earth, grazing with peace in His green pastures. But let me assure you of one thing, fellow Christ-followers, I have learned far more about my precious Lord and Savior in the valleys than I ever have on the mountaintops. I am exceedingly thankful for all that He has led me through to teach me and to allow me to experience Him and draw me ever so much closer to Him.

Let's conclude this chapter looking at some passages from 1 Peter. We want to understand that we are God's chosen and precious jewel but we will face tribulation and trials throughout our lives here on earth. Greater still is the assurance that our mighty and holy God will walk through them with us.

1 Peter 1:1-2, "Peter, an apostle of Jesus Christ, To those who reside as aliens, scattered throughout Pontus, Galatia, Cappadocia, Asia, and Bithynia, who are chosen according to the foreknowledge of God the Father, by the sanctifying work of the Spirit, to obey Jesus Christ and be sprinkled with His blood: May grace and peace be yours in the fullest measure."

Let us make sure that we understand who we are and whose we are so that we can fully understand our place here on earth. We are chosen by a holy God to walk in the fullness of Him. Sanctified through the blood of Jesus Christ so that we may have the fullest measure of the grace and peace that life in Him offers.

1 Peter 1:3-9, "Blessed be the God and Father of our Lord Jesus Christ, who according to His great mercy has caused us to be born again to a living hope through the resurrection of Jesus Christ from the dead, to obtain an inheritance which is imperishable and undefiled and will not fade away, reserved in heaven for you, who are protected by the power of God through faith for a salvation ready to be revealed in the last time. In this you greatly rejoice, even though now for a little while, if necessary, you have been distressed by various trials, so that the proof of your faith, being more precious than gold which is perishable, even though tested by fire, may be found to result in praise and glory and honor at the revelation of Jesus Christ; and though you have not seen Him, you love Him, and though you do not see Him now, but believe in Him, you greatly rejoice with joy inexpressible and full of glory, obtaining as the outcome of your faith the salvation of your souls."

Let's be sure to grip with a firm hold, the glory of God and the joy for us here. We should be able to praise God and give Him glory because of His grace and mercy for us that will one day result in heaven for us. Here on earth we will go through trials and be tested by fire but the results of our testings will be glory for God and a proving of our faith which results in salvation through Him. I can exceedingly rejoice because of the reward that is to come.

1 Peter 3:13-16, "Who is there to harm you if you prove zealous for what is good? But even if you should suffer for the sake of righteousness, you are blessed. AND DO NOT FEAR THEIR INTIMIDATION, AND DO NOT BE TROUBLED, but sanctify Christ as Lord in your hearts, always being ready to make a defense to everyone who asks you to give an account for the hope that is in you, yet with gentleness and reverence; and keep a good conscience so that in the thing in which you are slandered, those who revile your good behavior in Christ will be put to shame."

Peter gives us yet another view of the trials and tribulations that we might suffer. In America, we are just beginning to see this particular testing of our faith. We are beginning to see that being a Christian, can bring negative consequences and some of those consequences are beginning to be more difficult to accept. Yet we are to take every opportunity and give an account of our faith in God. When we go through trials and people watch us as we dig into our faith and trust in God, they then ask why or how do you walk through these terrible trials with your head held high? At that moment, we have the most precious and sacred opportunity to share God and His blood-bought grace and His perfect peace that comes through our faith. If our focus is on Christ, as it always should be, then we must always be prepared to give an account to others when they ask about our faith and our trust and our peace. Trials give us sacred opportunities to share Jehovah God, Jesus Christ, with others.

1 Peter 4:1-6, "Therefore, since Christ has suffered in the flesh, arm yourselves also with the same purpose, because he who has suffered in the flesh has ceased from sin, so as to live the rest of the time in the flesh no longer for the lusts of men, but for the will of God. For the time already past is sufficient for you to have carried out the desire of the Gentiles, having pursued a course of sensuality, lusts, drunkenness, carousing, drinking parties and abominable idolatries. In all this, they are surprised that you do not run with them into the same excesses of dissipation, and they malign you; but they will give account to Him who is ready to judge the living and the dead. For the gospel has for this purpose been preached even to those who are dead, that though they are judged in the flesh as men, they may live in the spirit according to the will of God."

Christ Himself suffered as a man here on this earth, therefore we must be prepared to suffer as well. This passage of scripture deals with being made fun of or being put down by our friends. People who do not KNOW God or have a relationship with

Jesus Christ will talk about you and make fun of you when you live your life completely sold out to your Savior. Peter reminds us that they will face the Father also and will give an account of why they put down or belittled His chosen ones. We can take heart in the fact that God will handle their words and actions and we don't have to be distraught over them. However, we should see them as Christ sees them and as He sees us. We must know that they do not have the faith we have and they probably do not have the assurance of salvation and they definitely are not walking in the Spirit. Therefore, He tells us in Matthew 5:44, we are to pray for those who persecute us so they may come to know salvation through Jesus Christ.

1 Peter 4:12-19, *"Beloved, do not be surprised at the fiery ordeal among you, which comes upon you for your testing, as though some strange thing were happening to you; but to the degree that you share the sufferings of Christ, keep on rejoicing, so that also at the revelation of His glory you may rejoice with exultation. If you are reviled for the name of Christ, you are blessed, because the Spirit of glory and of God rests on you. Make sure that none of you suffers as a murderer, or thief, or evildoer, or a troublesome meddler; but if anyone suffers as a Christian, he is not to be ashamed, but is to glorify God in this name. For it is time for judgment to begin with the household of God; and if it begins with us first, what will be the outcome for those who do not obey the gospel of God? AND IF IT IS WITH DIFFICULTY THAT THE RIGHTEOUS IS SAVED, WHAT WILL BECOME OF THE GODLESS MAN AND THE SINNER? Therefore, those also who suffer according to the will of God shall entrust their souls to a faithful Creator in doing what is right."*

Don't be surprised! If Jesus Christ suffered, so will we! No way around that truth. If we suffer for being a Christ-follower, then we will rejoice. However, Peter reminds us that sometimes we suffer because we choose sin. Sin will always bring suffering and there is no way around that truth either. But if we suffer in trials so that God may be glorified then we can rejoice always. Plain and simply we are to trust our Creator to know what is best for us. We must trust Him through every circumstance that He will take care of us. We must trust Him that He will use us to bring glory to Himself and to bring others to His kingdom. We must trust Him that in the end, we will sit at His feet and worship and walk the golden streets of heaven where there is no more pain and no more suffering.

It may seem hard to focus on trials and tribulations when we are looking for peace but when we understand that He will not leave us nor forsake us in the middle of those trials, we will have peace in the midst of the strongest gales and the darkest valleys. John 16:33 helps us to get and keep the right focus as we learn about having peace in the valleys. *"These things I have spoken to you, that in Me you may have peace. In the world you have tribulations, BUT take courage; I have overcome the world."* Jesus assures us that in the world we WILL have tribulations but take courage because He has overcome the world and we will have peace in Him in the midst of our trials.

CHAPTER TWO

Searching for Peace

Father God, You are the One who holds life and gives it abundantly to those of us who seek after You and find You through Jesus Christ our Savior and Lord and through the cross where He bore our sins and freely gave us mercy and grace and through Your Holy Spirit who brings us daily strength and wisdom and peace. Father, please allow this lesson to be Your Word speaking forth to the ones You have called to come to this place and time. Provide a hedge of protection around them as they encounter You and Your Word in these pages and prevent satan from pulling them away at points that may be uncomfortable. Hold them fast to Your Word so that they can find the everlasting peace that You and You alone give. Through the power of the cross and the resurrection and through the saving and life-giving name of Jesus Christ do I humbly ask these things. Amen and Amen!

Psalm 34:12-14, "Who is the man who desires life and loves length of days that he may see good? Keep your tongue from evil and your lips from speaking deceit. Depart from evil and do good; Seek peace and pursue it."

We cannot sit still and wish for peace, hoping that it will just pour over us.

Hebrews 12:14, "Pursue peace with all men, and the sanctification without which no one will see the Lord."

Look closely at the word, "pursue", so you can understand the starting point of this chapter. The New Oxford American Dictionary defines the word "pursue" as: to follow in order to catch or attack AND to continue or proceed (as along a path). We are to go after peace, to follow the path in order to catch peace. It will take effort and determination on our part. It will take moving away from things that deter us and moving toward God's Word that sustains us.

How does the world suggest that we pursue or find peace? We'll look at a few examples. First, advertising executives tell us moms that if we would purchase their bath products and go run a hot bath and light lots of candles and play some soothing music, we will find blissful peace. As most moms can testify, that peace may last ten minutes because as soon as you get comfortable and just begin to feel your muscles relax and seconds before your mind can even come to that relaxing and peaceful place, there is suddenly a knock at the door that demands you answer because it is most definitely an emergency that cannot wait one single minute. Even if you do get a full thirty minutes of relaxing in a warm bath, as soon as you open that door, life hits you full in the face. That peace was fleeting.

Another industry that knows "exactly" what we need is the tourism industry. They tell us to come to the beach. Lie on the white sand and listen to the waves gently rolling in and then slowly sliding off the shore. Hear the sound of the waves breaking near the shore and the seagulls searching for crumbs. Smell the splash and spray of the salt water. Bask in the warmth of the sun as all your troubles melt gently away. It is wonderful while you are there on that beach. However, as you begin packing up the car and get on the road headed home, you can already feel the anxiety beginning to creep back into your heart and mind. As you open the door of home, life again hits you square in the face and all the anxiety you left behind, comes rushing back and then you long for the beach even more and you begin to resent (even if just a little) the life you live is not on that beach. That peace was fleeting.

Realtors, who make a good living from the money spent on mountain cabins, entice you to come to the majesty of God's beautiful forests and mountain streams. Come spend a week and take long strolls through the forests and linger near the clear, cool mountain streams. You will hear the birds chirping as the water flows ever so gently over the rocks and cascades down the captivating waterfalls. Climb high to the mountain peaks and see as far as eye can wander and see the splendor and majesty of our mighty God's creation. (I have to admit here, this is one of my most relaxing places.) You are at peace, feeling no stress, BUT THEN, you have to pack up and go home. Most assuredly, the peace does not go home with you and what little bit might try to linger with you, does not stay for any length of time within your heart once you are at home. So again, we find ourselves longing for the mountains to find peace and we find a small nudging of resentment building inside of us knowing we cannot live in the peaceful mountain escape. That peace was fleeting.

Disney, experts at manipulating our emotions, tells us to come to the place where dreams come true and magic really does happen. Disney has done a tremendous amount of research on people's emotions and what controls people's psyche. They know how to convince you that fairy tales can come true if you come to Disney. They don't even play music by chance as you wait in line. The music and cadence of the rhythm have a purpose for whether they want you to be calm in long lines or to be excited as you enter a ride. The faster the beat and the louder the music, the more your heart rate increases and the more excited you get. The slower the beat and the softer the music, the more your heart rate decreases and the more peaceful you are. However, there is always noise as that is the controlling factor for the emotions of mass crowds. It keeps you going. Truth is we have so much fun in Disney as our emotions are controlled, we just can't wait to come back and spend more money. I was told by a co-worker several years ago, "I wish we could live in Disney, then my dysfunctional family would be just fine." Tragedy is that you can't live in Disney and her marriage ended in divorce. Disney is an escape from reality. If we need an escape from reality to function, then we really are in big trouble. We can't live at Disney. We must go back home to face the reality of our lives which is full of daily trials and tribulations. That peace was fleeting.

This last one may be the most disturbing to me from a spiritual viewpoint. If you are sad or you are having problems coping with life's circumstances – then just ask the doctor because there is a pill for that. Can't find rest, need more sleep, there are many pills for that and for some of those pills you don't even need a doctor to write a prescription. Please don't turn away if this makes you uncomfortable. Remember we are instructed to pursue peace so let's be brave enough to look at all the things that might be robbing us of that peace. I am one that lives through many sleepless night and have in the past been given pills to ease my pain and to help me sleep so I speak from absolute experience here. However, I believe all of us, at one time or another, may have turned too quickly to the pills so freely given to us to fix whatever is bothering us. There are accounts in the Bible where God woke someone up to pray or to read a Scripture that they would need that next day. I don't want to be in a medically induced sleep and not hear that still small voice or feel that gentle nudge when God wants me to move or listen or speak. Most of the sleeping medicines and the pain medicines linger in our systems. If we take them at night, the hangover feeling stays with us throughout the next day. It prevents us from having a sensitive spirit as we see others in need or we miss the brush of the Holy Spirit in our hearts and so we miss being a blessing and receiving a blessing in return. So many today are too quick to take anxiety pills when we are saddened by life's trials and tribulations. AND the doctors are ready with prescription pad in hand to write you as many pills as you want to help whatever feeling you are having. My best example of this is with my mom. At the time of this story, she had buried both her parents, her husband and two sons. She had survived two major heart attacks. She lived daily with acute knee pain. She had never depended upon any anxiety medication because she 100% depended upon her Heavenly Father as her Comforter and her Great Physician. At this particular time, she was being seen by a home health nurse and it was time for her re-evaluation. It was during cold and flu season and we wanted her to be able to be seen at home and have her weekly blood work done at home so she wouldn't be exposed to those germs if she had to go into the outpatient portion of the hospital. But she was improving and was doing "too well" to continue with home care. One of her nurses suggested that we call the doctor and tell him she is sad and then they could order her anxiety medicines and that would give them the reason to recertify her under their healthcare guidelines. I was floored and emphatically stated that NO we would not do that. All you have to do is tell the doctor you are sad more than a few days a month and he can write you anxiety medication. Our children are being medicated to sit still in school. College kids take pills to focus better. If you have an issue of any kind, there is a pill for that. WHERE is our dependence on God?!?!? We are a nation depending on pills to get us through life's circumstances. The pills don't bring lasting peace though because when they wear off, the issues are still there and one pill is usually not enough after a period of time and so you take two and then you need more after that. We run from the pain and anguish of our trials and tribulations but we run in the wrong direction. That peace is not only fleeting but is highly detrimental to our ability to find true and perfect peace.

Don't turn away at this point if you feel like I have stepped on your toes. I am not saying anything is sinful or bad about all of these tourist places. God Himself tells us we need to get away from people and circumstances to be renewed and encouraged in our journey so that we have the strength to move forward each day.

Matthew 14:23-24, "After He had sent the crowds away, He went up on the mountain by Himself to pray; and when it was evening, He was there alone."

This passage tells us that Jesus Himself, Son of God, the Holy One, as a human had to withdraw from everyone, even those closest to Him, to get away for a while to find some peaceful time. So, we too need to get away from our routines and find some time to rest and relax. However, the problem comes when we look to those places as our source of peace and we pursue peace there.

That peace does not last and does not have the power of Perfect Peace to carry us through life's trials and tribulations each and every day. Doctors cannot bring us lasting functional peace through any amount of pills. They only help satan force us to push God away and keep Him at a distance so that we don't have to deal with life. This is a deception of satan because all of us have to give an account of how we use every moment of time that God has given us. Therefore, we must look to the Word to find out how to get that Perfect Peace that we so desperately want and need. What peace are we to pursue? To go after? To follow along the path of life?

Numbers 6:24-27, "The Lord bless you, and keep you; The Lord make His face shine on you, And be gracious to you; The Lord lift up His countenance on you, And give you peace. So they shall invoke My name on the sons of Israel, and I then will bless them."

Where is my peace going to come from? It is going to come from God just as He promised to the nation of Israel, He will bring it to me if I pursue it faithfully. In Luke chapter 1, Zacharias is praising the Lord for the birth of his son John and for the miracles that God has shown him and he says this in verses 78-79, "Because of the tender mercy of our God, with which the Sunrise from on high shall visit us, to shine upon those who sit in darkness and the shadow of death, to guide our feet into the way of peace." He was praising his Heavenly Father, who was going to send the "Son"shine of heaven to guide our feet into the way of peace. Jesus was sent to show us the way of peace. If we want true, everlasting, strong dependable, able-to-withstand-any-trial or tribulation kind of peace, then we must look to Jesus, the Word who became flesh and dwelt among us.

Ephesians 2:13-17, "But now in Christ Jesus you who formerly were far off have been brought near by the blood of Christ. For He Himself is our peace, who made both groups into one and broke down the barrier of the dividing wall, by abolishing in His flesh the enmity, which is the Law of commandments contained in *ordinances, so that in Himself He might make the two into one new man, thus establishing peace, and might reconcile them both in one body to God through the cross, by it having put to death the enmity."*

If we want peace, we must have Jesus since He is our peace and the only way to get it is through the cross. We are going to cover this topic in depth in the next chapter. For now, we will continue to talk about having peace and then we will use the next several chapters to detail some of the specific items God says we must have in order to have everlasting peace. If you want to have the Perfect Peace that will be discussed here, then make sure you read the next chapter on repentance and make sure that you have trusted Jesus as Savior and Lord and developed a personal relationship with Him, because if not, you will not find peace in a formula or a basic lesson on how to live. If Jesus is not your personal Lord and Savior, there is no formula anywhere on this earth that you can follow to find Perfect Peace. Jesus, as Savior and Lord, is the foundation and the only life-giving fountain through which true peace flows.

Galatians 5:22-26, "But the fruit of the Spirit is love, joy, peace, patience, kindness, goodness, faithfulness, gentleness, self-control; against such things there is no law. Now those who belong to Christ Jesus have crucified the flesh with its passions and desires. If we live by the Spirit, let us also walk by the Spirit. Let us not become boastful, challenging one another, envying one another."

The fruit of the Spirit (the Spirit being the Holy Spirit that resides in us after we have asked Jesus to be our Savior and we have made Him Lord of our lives) is peace. As was stated earlier, you can't have this without Jesus Christ. Pay close attention to the rest of the verse. Those who belong to Christ Jesus have crucified the flesh with its passion and desires. So, let's start here. Have you really crucified your flesh and said no to its passions and desires? As God opens my eyes and lets me see from His viewpoint, I can answer for most of us and say no, not even close. If you want to hear the Word from God, then I ask you to stop right now and pray and ask God to open your heart and your mind to hear His Word. Bear through the rest of this chapter and continue to the end and then ask God to speak to your heart about whatever circumstance He is bringing to your mind. It may be hard but He wants to rid you of the things that are robbing you of that Perfect Peace.

As we choose the ways of the flesh, we try to put God on a shelf and we do not walk in the Spirit. When we pick up the flesh and walk in the flesh, then we lose peace and strength and power. Let's look at some real examples of what this means. At the end of the day did you make sure that you got all your work done, whether at home or at a professional job? Did you get the kids to dance, cheer, ball practice, music lessons, this club or that club? Did you and/or your spouse make every meeting and appointment that you had scheduled? Did you get to watch your favorite TV show(s)? Did you schedule time to see that new movie everyone is talking about? Did you respond to everyone's posts on facebook and make sure you read all the new tweets for the day? Did you remember to update your status? How much time did you have for yourself to play that new game you downloaded? Did you get everything ready for whatever hobby is your favorite to make sure that you were prepared for the recreational events of the weekend? Did you sit down with your child and/or your spouse to read the Word of God and pray together? Did you have time to discuss your child's emotional day and what he/she encountered that day? Did you have time over dinner to discuss with your spouse how his/her day went and to really care about what he/she encountered during the day? Where was dinner – at home in peace and quiet and time for family sharing or driving through a diner that offers the worst food possible for your body which is supposed to be the temple of God? Did you do your daily Bible reading and check it off your to-do list? When you balance your checkbook at the end of the month and you look at your individual expenses, how much money was spent on pleasures and desires for you and your family? (Remember that most recreational activities are desires and pleasures not needs) Has your peace not come because you have overscheduled every minute of every day and have left no time to sit at the feet of Jesus through His Word and through worship time to rest and gain strength through Him? Are you teaching your children that things and accomplishments of this world are more important than sitting at the feet of Jesus? Are you teaching your children that as long as you are not too late with payments then it is OK to spend what you want to have fun and to be entertained and to be popular and to do what everyone else is doing? Are you teaching your children that as long as you make an appearance at church on a regular basis and that you are "good people" that you are doing enough to be called a Christian? Is satan using the things of this world to drain the very life and peace out of you? Are you living your life in turmoil that you created yourself as satan and his demons stand by laughing at their victories? We are going to cover this topic in great detail in the last chapter so I'll leave it for now but I ask you to look at your schedule and look at your checkbook and see if there is any evidence that you have crucified your flesh. As you read the previous verse, remember, it doesn't say that if you ask Jesus to be your Savior then you will have peace. It says if we have asked Jesus to be Lord and Savior then we **WILL** crucify the flesh and if we live by the Spirit, we should walk by the Spirit and **THEN**, in this circumstance, the fruit, of living and walking by the Spirit, will be peace.

Philippians 4:1-5, *"Therefore, my beloved brethren whom I long to see, my joy and crown, in this way stand firm in the Lord, my beloved. I urge Euodia and I urge Syntyche to live in harmony in the Lord. Indeed, true companion, I ask you also to help these women who have shared my struggle in the cause of the gospel, together with Clement also and the rest of my fellow workers, whose names are in the book of life. Rejoice in the Lord always; again I will say, rejoice!"*

Paul is encouraging the believers in Philippi to do three things here. First, he tells them to stand firm in the Lord. If we are to pursue peace, we have to stand firm in the Lord. You better believe that as soon as you make the commitment to pursue peace, satan and his demons will rear their ugly heads and try to "show you" that this will never happen in your life. It might work for others, but it will not work for you. As I teach teenagers or adults in Bible study, I always tell them that no matter what the lesson, if God is moving in your heart about that particular lesson, you can KNOW that satan will pull out all the stops to come against you and try to discourage you. It will happen! There is no maybe or might happen. It WILL happen! So, if we know this before we even begin to set our mind on the pursuit of peace, then we won't be surprised when it happens and we will be able to have our defensive weapons ready. We need to have our swords ready to be drawn. Our sword is the Word of God. Jesus gave us the example of quoting Scripture to defeat satan as satan attempted to tempt Him in the wilderness. God says to resist the devil in Jesus' name and he will flee from you. There is power in the name of Jesus. Speak it aloud and refuse to give satan one moment of your time or of your peace. It is time we as Christ followers, take the power and authority that is given to us in the name of Jesus and through the power of the Holy Spirit who lives in us. Set your mind and stand firm in the Lord and put satan in his place.

Second, Paul told the Philippians to live in harmony in the Lord. We are going to look at this one deeper in a later lesson because relationships seem to rob our peace more than anything else. For now, let's just take a peek at how this should look in our lives. At this point, at least one or two of you will say but you don't know the people in my life that create drama and turmoil. If we are honest, we all have people who make it difficult to live in harmony. Satan convinces us that they need to change and that it is all their fault. Christ tells us to get the log out of our own eye before we try to get the speck out of the eye of our offender. To pursue peace that God wants to give us, we must determine how we are going to change our perception and our reactions to each situation. Before we continue, make a list of the people who cause you the most trials and tribulations. Keep this before you as you study God's Word. Talk to Him about these people. Tell Him honestly (remember – He already knows your heart so there is really nothing you can hide) that you don't like that person – at all – not one little bit. Tell Him why you don't like that person – give details and examples. Then allow Him, give Him permission, to soften your heart. Tell Him that you don't have the power or even the desire to like that person or you have no desire to live in harmony with that person but that you KNOW that He can change your heart. Ask Him to do a work in YOUR heart. Anytime we go to God, change is about us not the other person. This is a critical point to keep in mind and it is hard to accept when "that person" is the one who satan throws at us every day. I have had many of "those people" in my life and I still do. Just about the time I work my heart and mind and my grace and my attitude out about one person another quickly pops up. It's like playing whack-a-mole. They just keep popping up in all different areas of my life. Yes, I really do understand how difficult this one is to adjust in your life. But remember, God is greater, if we will trust Him and His ways, even in relationships, He will bring us to perfect peace.

Third, Paul tells the Philippians to help others who struggle in the cause of the gospel and whose names are in the book of life. I had a small book years ago entitled, "The Blessing is in the Doing." I no longer have it and I don't remember the author's name but the short message was powerful. It stated that you can't sit and be blessed. You have to get up and do something and then you will be blessed. Well, I believe the same premise works here. You can't sit and find peace. You have to set aside your wants and complaints and get up and help others. In helping others and focusing on their needs, your wants and worries fade away. I can look at my squash and zucchini harvest from last year and complain and get frustrated because I was only able to put up ten bags when I wanted to put up 30-40 bags. Then I can go take a meal to a widow and look in her cupboard and see that she has one can of soup and one can of tuna to last her a week. My complaining will go rapidly away as I put my focus on helping others. Through this process, you find that most of your worries and anxiety was over worthless things and that in finding a more important purpose as you follow God's lead, you find greater peace as He upholds you and sustains you as you help others.

Philippians 4:4-10, "Rejoice in the Lord always; again I will say, rejoice! Let your gentle spirit be known to all men. The Lord is near. Be anxious for nothing, but in everything by prayer and supplication with thanksgiving let your requests be made known to God. And the peace of God, which surpasses all comprehension, will guard your hearts and your minds in Christ Jesus. Finally, brethren, whatever is true, whatever is honorable, whatever is right, whatever is pure, whatever is lovely, whatever is of good repute, if there is any excellence and if anything worthy of praise, dwell on these things. The things you have learned and received and heard and seen in me, practice these things, and the God of peace will be with you."

This passage is packed full of simple instructions about finding peace. Paul gives us easy to understand, easy to enact, practical instructions and tells us specifically what to do in order to receive that perfect peace that only God can provide.

BE ANXIOUS FOR NOTHING – I have heard it said that worry indicates a lack of trust in God's wisdom, sovereignty and power. I believe that to be true. If I can sit and watch a movie in my house while a thunderstorm is passing over, I trust that my house will protect me and I am not fearful of it blowing away. The thunderstorm may be raging around me, but I can trust my house to keep me safe and dry. I certainly would be aware of the storm around me but I would not panic and I would not run to someone else's house with the hope of being safer there. When the storms are raging in my life, I need to trust that God is wise and sovereign and powerful. If my physical house blows away in the storm, I have to trust that God will lead me to the resources that will once again provide me with shelter. If my physical body is destroyed by disease I must trust that God will give me a new glorified body when I leave this earth and enter the glory of heaven. With lesser storms than these, I MUST trust God. I can't give up and run to someone else's philosophy or ideas. I must trust God and the instruction of His Word.

IN EVERYTHING - by prayer and supplication – with thanksgiving – let your requests be made known to God. The storm is coming. You see it on the horizon. You feel the eerie calm before the storm. The air pressure is dropping and you can feel the imminent danger approaching. You feel your heart rate increase. What do you do? Who do you call? We as humans are social beings. We usually pick up the phone and call those closest to us. We tell everyone who will listen. We post it in large letters on social media so every one of our "friends" can see our trials. The problem is they cannot fix your problems. They cannot stop the storm. Or you may be more like me, when I see the storm approaching, I go into solution mode. I want to quickly evaluate the problem and develop the solution in my own ability with my own knowledge. I don't really have the wisdom to accurately fix my problems. I don't have the power to stop the storm! Our first response to any trial, no matter how large or how small, should ALWAYS be to fall to our knees in prayer to the all-powerful, all-knowing, all-present Jehovah God. When we pray we are to begin with thanksgiving. This is a difficult response if we are not walking in the Spirit of God. When the doctor said those three life-altering words to my husband, "it is cancer", did we really have anything to be thankful for? When we learned that it was exactly the same cancer that took my brother 15 years prior in only eight months after his diagnosis, did we really have anything to be thankful for in our prayers of desperation? YES! We most certainly did! We thanked God for being there in that doctor's office with us. We thanked Him for the promise that He would never leave us nor forsake us. We thanked Him for the salvation and grace that He so lavishly poured over both of us long before that moment in our journeys of life. Every day we thanked Him for provisions and His Word that offered such hope and comfort! How could we do that you ask? Because long before those words were uttered, we both had the assurance that in death, we would lose these old broken bodies but we would receive glorified bodies and be immediately swept away to the glory of heaven. When we declare thanksgiving in the middle of our trials, peace is ushered in to the depths of our hearts and we have the strength to go on through the darkness of the valley as we keep our eyes on the light. Even in our sufferings we can find thankfulness if we look for it. This life on earth is an infinitesimally small dot in the scope of eternity. I may suffer for a little while, but the glory of my mansion and the streets of gold and the pure pleasure of sitting at my Savior's feet for eternity is far greater than any suffering I can do on this earth and for that I can ALWAYS be thankful. Talk to Him first and thank HIM for His love and grace and mercy and strength that He pours out on you each day.

SET YOUR MIND – Paul lists the things we should think about throughout our days. To find that peace that guards our hearts and our minds, we must decide what we will think about. It is a choice and we must determine what our choice will be. Let me challenge you to take a survey of your day. Start by listing how much time you spent watching TV or on electronic devices. Evaluate the TV programs that you watched and the social media you participated in. How much was honoring to God? How much was uplifting to your spirit? What did you read today? What did your conversations consist of with others? Were you talking about God and lifting others up or were you tearing others down? Even when we give time to listen to others who are sharing gossip, we become a part of that gossip. You must learn to be tactful and refuse to listen. Either stop the conversation or walk away from any conversation that is not bringing glory to God through your words or your participation. Notice I didn't say to walk away from the conversation you didn't want to be a part of. BECAUSE from our sinful nature, too many of us really want to be in the middle of those gossipy conversations. We must determine that we will not. This is work but remember we are pursuing peace. We are going after it, working for it. This is a part of the work that we must do. We will cover more details about this in the chapter about reining in our thoughts and actions but for now realize that peace does not come as the world offers it, it comes only as we align our lives with the Word of God.

Philippians 4:10-20, "But I rejoiced in the Lord greatly, that now at last you have revived your concern for me; indeed, you were concerned before, but you lacked opportunity. Not that I speak from want, for I have learned to be content in whatever circumstances I am. I know how to get along with humble means, and I also know how to live in prosperity; in any and every circumstance I have learned the secret of being filled and going hungry, both of having abundance and suffering need. I can do all things through Him who strengthens me. Nevertheless, you have done well to share with me in my affliction. You yourselves also know, Philippians, that at the first preaching of the gospel, after I left Macedonia, no church shared with me in the matter of giving and receiving but you alone; for even in Thessalonica you sent a gift more than once for my needs. Not that I seek the gift itself, but I seek for the profit which increases to your account. But I have received everything in full and have an abundance; I am amply supplied, having received from Epaphroditus what you have sent, a fragrant aroma, an acceptable sacrifice, well-pleasing to God. And my God will supply all your needs according to His riches in glory in Christ Jesus."

For most of us we have many wants and very few needs. We live in a nation of abundance. Maybe there are times that God takes us to a place of living in need so that we can better appreciate living with wants. Paul said that he learned to be content in whatever circumstances he was in at the time. To find the lasting peace that we long for, we have to learn to be content in whatever circumstances that we are in at the moment. One big problem for us in this area is the multi-billion-dollar advertising industry. Companies get paid big bucks, really big bucks, to convince us that we do not have all that we "need". We are bombarded from TV, magazines, emails, billboards, text messages, phone calls, social media ads, etc., telling us that we do not have all that we need. If we would purchase their product, our lives would be sooooooooooo much better. We watch "reality" shows of the famous and rich and tell ourselves that we are poor because we don't have this or that. We see the opulent indulgence of fools and long to have what they have. We blame our parents for not giving us enough. We blame our spouses for not giving us more. We blame our jobs for not paying enough so we can have more. And then the greatest tragedy is that we put that attitude into our children. Many children today have more stuff by the age of ten, than many young adults had 15 years ago. I watch with horror and a broken heart as young children stomp their feet and demand the latest cell phone or new gaming system. My heart doesn't break because they demand it but because the parents go in debt and purchase it for them and say, "What was I supposed to do? All her friends have it already. I don't want her to feel left out." I could stay on this topic for a long time but I will save it for the last chapter. Do you want the peace of God? Learn to say, "That is not a need" and, "No, you cannot have that!" Then learn to be content in whatever circumstances you are in at the moment and teach your children to do the same. Here's a hint though – get rid of the electronics and turn off the TV.

2 Peter 3:14-18, "Therefore, beloved, since you look for these things, be diligent to be found by Him in peace, spotless and blameless, and regard the patience of our Lord as salvation; just as also our beloved brother Paul, according to the wisdom given him, wrote to you, as also in all his letters, speaking in them of these

things, in which are some things hard to understand, which the untaught and unstable distort, as they do also the rest of the Scriptures, to their own destruction. You therefore, beloved, knowing this beforehand, be on your guard so that you are not carried away by the error of unprincipled men and fall from your own steadfastness, but grow in the grace and knowledge of our Lord and Savior Jesus Christ. To Him be the glory, both now and to the day of eternity. Amen."

Be diligent to be found by Him in peace, spotless and blameless. Are you going after peace? Will you pursue it? There is a warning that follows and we need to closely heed the warning. As I stated earlier, if you determine to PURSUE peace with all your heart and all your mind and all your soul, satan will not sit idly by, but he will come after you to destroy the work of the Lord in your life. Stand firm and recognize that there will be people who will say not to take the Bible so seriously, sadly some of these people will be your church friends. Peter warns us that some things are hard to understand and that the untaught (not taught by the Spirit) and the unstable distort the Word and that this leads to destruction. He teaches us that we know this so be on guard lest we are carried away by the error of unprincipled men. Grow in grace and knowledge of our Lord and Savior Jesus Christ. Study and see for yourself what the Bible says. If you lack wisdom, ask and the Spirit of God will bring understanding to you. If you say that you are just going to do what everyone else is doing because everyone else can't possibly be wrong, then you need to take a careful look at this next passage.

Matthew 7:13-15, "Enter through the narrow gate; for the gate is wide and the way is broad that leads to destruction, and there are many who enter through it. For the gate is small and the way is narrow that leads to life, and there are few who find it."

Jesus teaches us not to follow the crowd on the wide road. Get on the narrow road that leads to life. That is the only way you will find peace. The trouble here is those little five-minute feel-good devotions cannot sustain you when the waves are crashing in on you and the darkness looms ever so closely in the valley. Wisdom of the WORD brings peace because you can speak the life of the WORD over your circumstances. In today's fast paced world, we want to be spoon fed instead of doing our own studying and we are being led as dumb little sheep to the slaughter as we buy into every false doctrine and wind of trickery that is being spewed out.

If we want peace, we must receive Jesus Christ as our Savior and relinquish all of our life, every part of it, to His Lordship. We must crucify our flesh and determine to control our minds and thoughts and look to God and His infallible Word for our daily guidance. If you find yourself longing for the deep peace that has been discussed here, please continue with me through this journey as we go back and take each of these topics and delve more deeply into each one. True peace can come and stay with you if you look to Jehovah God and His holy Word. The trials don't leave but the peace holds us and bears us up during the darkest times.

John 14:25-30, "These things I have spoken to you while abiding with you. But the Helper, the Holy Spirit, whom the Father will send in My name, He will teach you all things, and bring to your remembrance all that I said to you. Peace I leave with you; My peace I give to you; not as the world gives do I give to you. Do not let your heart be troubled, nor let it be fearful. You heard that I said to you, 'I go away, and I will come to you.' If you loved Me, you would have rejoiced because I go to the Father, for the Father is greater than I. Now I have told you before it happens, so that when it happens, you may believe."

The words of Jesus Christ Himself tells us that He leaves His peace with us but that His peace is not the same as the world's peace. Trust Him. Trust His Word.

Rom 8:6, "For the mind set on the flesh is death, but the mind set on the Spirit is life and peace"

Do you want peace? Do you really want peace? Set your mind on the Spirit. Find life and peace through Jesus Christ and His Word.

CHAPTER THREE

Coming to Repentance

Lord, God the Almighty, You reign in majesty and glory and Your holiness illumines all of the heavens. You are worthy of our praise and adoration. Because we are a sinful people, we can only see Your holiness through the blood of Your Son, Jesus Christ. Precious Lord, allow us to see clearly through this study what the sacrifice on the cross meant and what our response must be in order to gain salvation that allows us to live eternally in heaven with You. Let the Holy Spirit speak TRUTH, YOUR TRUTH, to our hearts through the Word and help us to have wise discernment to understand the full intention of Your Word as it is clearly written for us to understand and respond.

Description of Heaven from selected verses in Revelation Chapters 4 and 21:

"And he who was sitting on the throne was like a jasper stone and a sardius in appearance and there was a rainbow around the throne, like an emerald in appearance… from the throne proceed flashes of lightning and sounds and peals of thunder…. Before the throne there was as it were a sea of glass like crystal; the new Jerusalem has a great and high wall, with twelve gates, the wall of the city has twelve foundation stones, the material of the wall was jasper, and the city was pure gold and like clear glass, the foundation stones of the city wall were adorned with every kind of precious stone. The twelve gates were twelve pearls, each gate was a single pearl; the streets of the city were pure gold, like transparent glass. There was no temple, for the Lord God, the Almighty, and the Lamb are its temple, the city has no need for the sun or the moon to shine upon it for the glory of God has illumined it."

John gave the best description that he could give for a vision that was beyond and above anything his human mind could comprehend. Let's try to get the best vision we can get. Every object we see, including the foundation, or ground, is made of pure gold and everything is covered with the finest of jewels. The gate to the city is pure pearl. The illumination comes directly from God. There is no temple or church building for the living temple is there for us to worship. We will be standing around the throne that has lightning and thunder flashing forth from a backdrop of a rainbow of brilliance. We, with many others, will be worshiping our God. No crying, no pain, no cancer, no drug or alcohol abuse, no physical abuse, no emotional abuse, no hatred, no anger, no fear, no stealing, no killing, no adulterers, no selfishness, no depression, no indulgences – none of this will exist in Heaven. We will be in resurrected bodies worshiping before the throne of God. What a picture!!! Don't you want to go right now!!

The Description of Hell

We have looked at Heaven and now we will look at hell because eternity for every human being that has lived before us, is now living or is yet to live, will be spent in one of the two places. There is no alternative! We must understand and make the right decision.

Isaiah 33:14, "Sinners in Zion are terrified; trembling has seized the godless. Who among us can live with the consuming fire? Who among us can live with continual burning?"

Mark 9:43-44, "And if your hand causes you to stumble, cut it off; it is better for you to enter life crippled, than having your two hands, to go into hell, into the unquenchable fire, [where their worm does not die, and the fire is not quenched]"

Luke 16:23-24, "And in Hades he lifted up his eyes, being in torment, and saw Abraham far away, and Lazarus in his bosom. And he cried out and said, 'Father Abraham, have mercy on me, and send Lazarus that he may dip the tip of his finger in water and cool off my tongue; for I am in agony in this flame.'"

Matthew 8:12, "but the sons of the kingdom shall be cast out into the outer darkness; in that place there shall be weeping and gnashing of teeth."

2 Thessalonians 1:9, "And these will pay the penalty of eternal destruction, away from the presence of the Lord and from the glory of His power."

Revelation 19:20, "And the beast was seized, and with him the false prophet who performed the signs in his presence, by which he deceived those who had received the mark of the beast and those who worshiped his image; these two were thrown alive into the lake of fire which burns with brimstone."

Revelation 21:8, "But for the cowardly and unbelieving and abominable and murderers and immoral persons and sorcerers and idolaters and all liars, their part will be in the lake that burns with fire and brimstone, which is the second death."

Using the information from these verses we see that hell is a horrible place to even imagine. When we think about burning in hell, let's consider what a burn is like. Have you ever burned your arm or any part of your body? The initial pain is bad but the lingering pain through the healing process can be extremely painful. Burns are so awful that they require special treatment and wound care. Most of us know how much pain a single burn on our hand can be. BUT can you imagine every inch of your body burning all at the same time? The suffering in hell will be constant with no relief and it will be horrendous with no escape. There will be no relief from the burning. Everyone there will be angry with gnashing teeth. The picture I see in this is rabid animals. Animals that are rabid are mad, crazy, and beast-like. They bare their teeth in the attack mode. This is the picture of the humans in hell. The agony and anger and pain will be unrelenting for eternity. There will be no end to the suffering. There will be no place to hide from the suffering. There will be no one to comfort you in the suffering. Above all this, there will be eternal separation from God. There will be NO hope of change or help. Forever in torment separated from the only Hope of God. When you read through some studies on psychological profiles, you find that the human mind and body can live through extraordinary circumstances if there is a hope for something better. However, when one gives up hope or believes there is no hope, that person will die. You can see this in cancer patients. Those who have a strong belief or hope have a far greater chance of recovery. Yet, those who have no hope die much quicker in their cancer journey. In hell, there will be no hope but there will be no end. The lament to die will be forever but death from the torment will never come.

Now we have two Biblically described places to spend eternity. There is no other choice. So, I ask you the question – where do you want to spend eternity? It shouldn't take you long to decide that you want to spend eternity in Heaven. So how do we get there?

John 3:16, "For God so loved the world that He gave His only begotten Son, that whoever believes in Him, should not perish, but have eternal life."

According to this verse, all I have to do is believe in Jesus. Do you believe that Jesus was real? Do you believe that He was a great teacher? Do you believe that He was the promised Messiah? Do you believe that He was the Son of God incarnate? Do you believe that He is God? Do you believe that He was the sacrifice on the cross for your sins? Well if we stopped here, then getting to heaven would seem to be somewhat easy right? We even have multitudes of preachers and teachers today that say just repeat after me and say this memorized prayer and that's it, you're saved. I have seen well-meaning, seemingly intelligent, preachers herd a group of children down the aisle at Vacation Bible Schools and report to the church that all have accepted Jesus and believe on Him. I have enough knowledge to know how to manipulate a group of preschoolers and have them repeat words after me so they could tell everyone they are going to heaven. One very personal experience that I have had with this is through my grandniece. She attended a VBS and the leaders called her mother and told her she had prayed the prayer of salvation and they wanted to baptize her that night. We all said no that we needed to question her further. As we very carefully encouraged her to share her experience without us guiding her speech, she told us they said pray this prayer and she did. She had no concept of salvation even though she believed that God is real and that Jesus is the Messiah. Oh, how we need to be careful in how we handle the Word of God, as God gives strong discouragement to anyone who might lead one of His little ones astray. We must take the whole counsel of the Word of God.

James 2:19, "You believe that God is one. You do well; the demons also believe, and shudder."

OH NO!! What do we do now? The Bible says that the demons also believe that God is God and they shudder. And we know from the full counsel of the Word that the demons will spend eternity in hell. So now what am I to believe?

Salvation, that gets us to heaven, is not a head knowledge belief that God exists and that Jesus is His Son who came to live on earth and who died on a cross and then returned to heaven. Satan, himself, believes and knows that God is God and that Jesus is the Son of God who came to live a life on earth and died on the cross and arose after the third day and returned to heaven and then sent the Holy Spirit to live within each of us who have given our lives to Him. We know Satan won't be going to heaven – the Bible is very clear on that fact. So, what's the difference?

Let me give you another example – It is a scientific fact that my body needs water to live. I have learned about it in health class and I have read about it and studied about it as I have tried to learn about healthy living. I KNOW a lot about the need for water and the right kind of water to drink. I know that every cell in my body must have sufficient water every day or they will die. All of this knowledge does me absolutely no good if I don't drink the water. I can have gallons of alkalinized water sitting on my counter. I can purchase the most expensive water filtration system in the world. I can teach everyone about the importance of water. But until, I drink the water and get it inside of me, it will do NO good for my body. I must take the water into my body on a daily basis. Drinking water one day does not keep my body healthy. I must know and drink the water every day. As with God, I must first KNOW about Him and then I must take Him in through faith into my heart and I must feed my spiritual body with the Word every day. Knowing is just not enough to sustain me or to save me. I must move from knowledge to REPENTANCE.

2 Chronicles 7:14, "if My people who are called by My name humble themselves and pray, and seek My face and turn from their wicked ways, then I will hear from heaven, will forgive their sin, and will heal their land."

In this if/then statement, there are several actions clearly stated that we must do before God will hear and forgive. 1) Humble ourselves, 2) Pray, 3) Seek God, and 4) Turn away from our wicked ways. There is action required on our part.

Let's first look at the definition of repentance as defined in the Holman Illustrated Bible Dictionary (1995, Nashville). Change of mind; also can refer to regret or remorse accompanying realization that wrong has been done or to any shift or reversal of thoughts. In its Biblical sense repentance refers to a deeply seated and thorough turning from self to God. It occurs when a radical turning to God takes place – an experience which God is recognized as the most important fact of one's existence.

The Dictionary of Biblical Imagery, (1998, IVP, Illinois), gives us a great outline using Psalm 51 to teach us about true repentance.

Step 1 to repentance is to recognize the wrongs we have done. Genuine repentance begins with a clear understanding of the wrong committed.

Step 2 to repentance is cleansing sought with earnest grief.

Step 3 to repentance is true repentance brings a new desire for God.

Step 4 to repentance is that true repentance brings a changed action. Changed action is the most tangible demonstration of repentance – large strides in a new direction are the surest sign that repentance has occurred.

Let's take each of these steps through Psalm 51 and look at them more closely and apply them to our personal lives.

Psalm 51:1-5, "Be gracious to me, O God, according to Thy lovingkindness; according to the greatness of Thy compassion blot out my transgressions. Wash me thoroughly from my iniquity, and cleanse me from my sin. For I know my transgressions, and my sin is ever before me. Against Thee, Thee only, I have sinned. And done what is evil in Thy sight, so that Thou art justified when Thou dost speak, and blameless when Thou dost judge. Behold I was brought forth in iniquity, and in sin my mother conceived me."

Step 1 to repentance is to recognize the wrongs we have done. Genuine repentance begins with a clear understanding of the wrong committed.

We must do an evaluation of our hearts and allow the Holy Spirit to show us the sins (wrongs) we have committed. We must agree with God through the Holy Spirit that, yes, indeed, the actions or thoughts were/are sin.

Isaiah 64:6, "For all of us have become like one who is unclean and all our righteous deeds are like filthy garments..."

We should see us as God sees us in order to recognize our sins and how filthy they are to a Holy God.

Romans 3:23, "For all have sinned and fall short of the glory of God." I John 1:8, "If we say that we have no sin, we are deceiving ourselves and the truth is not in us."

No one that has ever lived or is living now or will live in the future will be without sin on this earth. The only exception to that statement is Jesus Christ who lived as all-God and all-man while He lived in human form on earth and He was without sin so that He could become our sacrifice.

Stop here and begin to write a list of sins in your life. Ask the Holy Spirit to reveal them to you and allow this to be an ongoing list so that as He reveals sin to you, you can write it down and deal with it, confessing it to God so that you can be cleansed from all your sin. Don't know where to start, start with the Ten Commandments in Exodus 20, then go to Matthew 5-7 and look at the teachings of Jesus and see where you measure up and where there is sin. Here is an example of why you should go to both passages to evaluate the sin in your life.

Exodus 20:13, "You shall not murder."

This is the law of the Ten Commandments. In the New Testament, Jesus says that He came not to abolish the law of the Old Testament but to explain it and fulfill it. Matthew 5:21 explains further the law of 'you shall not murder'. *"You have heard that the ancients were told, 'You shall not commit murder' and 'Whoever commits murder shall be liable to the court.' But I say to you that everyone who is angry with his brother shall be guilty before the court; and whoever shall say to his brother, 'Raca'(which means 'empty headed' or good for nothing') shall be guilty before the supreme court; and whoever shall say, 'you fool' shall be guilty enough to go into the fiery hell."* Jesus is teaching that we can murder someone's character with our words. He teaches that murder of someone's character is just as wrong as taking someone's physical life. When we get serious about seeing ourselves as Jesus sees us, then we will be ready to repent and seek forgiveness and redemption from God. Don't just hit the high points; allow God to get into the deep dark crevices of your mind and heart. It is important for us to remember here that sin is missing the mark that God set before us. It is not just what we are doing wrong but it is also what we know are requirements of God and not doing what is right. For instance, if God tells us to feed the hungry and we do nothing, even though doing nothing appears to others as we are doing nothing wrong, to God it is sin of disobedience.

Psalm 51:6-9, "Behold, Thou dost desire truth in the innermost being, and in the hidden part Thou wilt make me know wisdom. Purify me with hyssop, and I shall be clean; wash me, and I shall be whiter than snow. Make me to hear joy and gladness, let the bones which Thou hast broken rejoice. Hide Thy face from my sins, and blot out all my iniquities."

Step 2 to repentance is cleansing sought with earnest grief.

Once you become aware of sin, you should go through a period of wanting to become clean and to have your heart purified through the blood of Jesus. Hebrews 9:22 tells us that without the shedding of blood there is no forgiveness of sin. Ephesians 1:7 tells us that we have redemption through His blood. During this part of repentance, we are seeking redemption, forgiveness of our sins. Through redemption and forgiveness we are cleansed.

Let's take a moment here to understand why the shedding of blood was necessary to cover our sins. Not very long after God created Adam and Eve, through the temptations of Satan and the weakness of Eve and Adam, sin entered the world.

Genesis 3:21, "And the Lord God made garments of skin for Adam and his wife, and clothed them."

This was both a physical covering for their bodies as they had discovered their nakedness through sin and it was a spiritual covering for the sin. God took an innocent animal and shed its blood to cover the sin of Adam and Eve. The animal had nothing to do with the sin. We know that at that time the animal was perfect without stain and without deformity. For it to be a covering for Adam and Eve it had to die and its blood was shed. God gave the law as stated in the book of Leviticus, He stated that an animal for sacrifice had to be perfect without blemish. He was telling man that he had to sacrifice the best that he had to atone for his sins. All of this was looking forward to what God Himself was going to do when He gave His very best, in His Son Jesus Christ, by sending His perfect Son, who was without sin, to die on an old rugged cross and shed His precious blood because of my sin and your sin. When I recognize my sin and seek cleansing and forgiveness, I need to clearly see my Savior suffering on the cross and allowing His blood to spill down that cross as a covering and sacrifice for my sin. According to Romans 6:23, *"For the wages of sin is death, but the free gift of God is eternal life in Christ Jesus our Lord."* You and I deserve eternal death in a horrible hell. We deserve to be separated forever from God who is holy and perfect and full of grace and mercy. We can't blame our sin away on our parents, our circumstances, our society, or on Adam and Eve who were the first to sin. We absolutely must take responsibility and admit our sinful condition. When we sin, we should feel a ping in our heart that resembles the ping of the hammer as it drove the nails through our precious Savior's hands and feet as He shed His blood for us as a sacrifice to cover our sins.

Stop here and ask Him to forgive you of the list of sins that you wrote down. Lay your sins before Him and allow Him to be your sacrifice and allow Him to cover your sins with His blood. Tell Him you are sorry and ask Him to forgive and heal your heart. Stand on the promise of I John 1:9, *"If we confess our sins, He is **faithful** and **righteous** to forgive us our sins and to cleanse us from all unrighteousness."*

Psalm 51:10-12, *"Create in me a clean heart, O God, and renew a steadfast spirit within me. Do not cast me away from Thy presence, and do not take Thy Holy Spirit from me. Restore to me the joy of Thy salvation, and sustain me with a willing spirit."*

Step 3 – True repentance brings a new desire for God.

If I have recognized my sin and earnestly sought forgiveness from God then I will desire to be closer to God and I will long to be in His presence. The first two steps can be easy, especially if we are caught doing something wrong and then we want to be forgiven; but true repentance makes us long for God's presence from which sin separates us. It is hard for most Americans to understand what longing really means. We say we are tired of waiting when we have been waiting for 10 minutes at a fast food restaurant. We want something for a couple of months and we say we are longing to have that item. True longing comes when we lose a loved one and we hurt deeply as we long to be in that person's presence. That is the type of longing that we should have for God - to want to be in His presence more than anything else during the day or during the night.

Isaiah 59:1-2, "Behold, the Lord's hand is not so short that it cannot save; neither is His ear so dull that it cannot hear. But your iniquities have made a separation between you and your God, and your sins have hidden His face from you, so that He does not hear."

True repentance should bring us back to that place of longing to be in the presence of God. We recognize that sin separates us from God and prevents Him from hearing us when we cry out to Him. This understanding makes us long to be forgiven and we want to be in the presence and hearing of our holy God.

Psalm 51:13-15, "Then I will teach transgressors Thy ways, and sinners will be converted to Thee. Deliver me from blood-guiltiness, O God, Thou God of my salvation; then my tongue will joyfully sing of Thy righteousness. O Lord, open my lips, that my mouth may declare Thy praise."

Step 4 – True repentance brings a changed action. Changed action is the most tangible demonstration of repentance – large strides in a new direction are the surest sign that repentance has occurred.

If true repentance has happened, then there is a changed action on our part. There must be a change in our thought patterns and/or a change in our actions. If we say we repent and then keep doing the same thing, then there has never been true repentance. I had someone in my life that would say ugly, hurtful things without thinking about what she was saying and then every time, after she had time to think about what she had said, she would come back and apologize. I finally told her not to come and apologize to me anymore because if she was truly sorry she would stop doing it. She felt bad later and she was truly sorry, at that moment when she said she was sorry, but she was never sorry enough to change her action. If we are repentant there must be change.

A pastor friend of mine uses a great analogy to help us understand this concept of being forgiven and being saved and yet after salvation we will still sin and need daily forgiveness. Before we are saved through the grace and blood of Jesus Christ, we are on a road headed to hell. We don't recognize our sin and we don't care about Jesus or seeing ourselves through His eyes. When He comes to us and reveals our sins to us for the very first time and shows us how to have salvation through Him, He picks us up, turns us around and puts us on the road that leads to heaven. We are now going in a totally different direction. We will never get back on the old road. However, there are ditches and detours on our road that is leading us to heaven. When we sin after we are saved, it is like running off the road and getting stuck in the ditch. We need other Christians to come along beside us and help us get out of that ditch and put us back on the road that brings blessings and joy as we walk toward God. Sometimes, we go so far as to take a detour. We still are not back on the road headed to hell but we are on a detour that takes us away from the blessings and holiness of God. We pray and ask God to forgive us and put us back on the road of blessings and joy. When we ask for forgiveness, He is faithful to forgive and cleanse us from all unrighteousness and to pick us up and help us along our journey in life. A changed action must happen after our repentance and forgiveness. If our repentance is genuine, we will not want to go back to that sin that separates us from God.

Romans 8:6, "For the mind set on the flesh is death, but the mind set on the Spirit is life and peace."

Let us set our mind on the Spirit through His Word to see what it teaches about repentance. We are going to use John the Baptist to better understand the message of repentance.

Luke 1:76-79, "And you, child, will be called the prophet of the Most High; for you will go on before the Lord to prepare His ways; to give to His people the knowledge of salvation by the forgiveness of their sins, because of the tender mercy of our God, with which the Sunrise from on high shall visit us, to shine upon those who sit in darkness and the shadow of death, to guide our feet into the way of peace."

This statement is from Zacharias, the father of John the Baptist. John the Baptist would be the forerunner of Jesus who would announce His coming. John would go before and make sure the people had knowledge of their sins and be ready to receive forgiveness from Jesus because of the mercy of God. Just as John the Baptist came to bring knowledge of sin and lead them to Christ, so the written Word of God does the same for us today. We must read the Word and listen to the prompting of the Spirit to identify our sins and to confess them before God and receive His forgiveness, whether this is the first time which leads to salvation or if this is daily cleansing from sin that keeps us in the presence of God.

Matthew 3:1-5, "Now in those days John the Baptist came, preaching in the wilderness of Judea, saying, 'REPENT for the kingdom of heaven is at hand.' For this is the one referred to by Isaiah the prophet, saying, 'The voice of the one crying in the wilderness, make ready the way of the Lord, make His paths straight!' Now John himself had a garment of camel's hair, and a leather belt about his waist; and his food was locusts and wild honey. Then Jerusalem was going out to him, and all Judea, and all the district around the Jordan."

John was not your suit and tie kind of guy. He was like a wild man with a strong passion to preach repentance to the people. He was not preaching in the towns or in the synagogue, which was the church of that day. He knew that what was being preached in the synagogues was not the true message of God and unfortunately, we see way too much of that today. As he preached with passion, the people came out to him. They heard about his powerful message and came from all over to hear him and to receive his message. He made sure that in his preaching, he ALWAYS pointed the people to Jesus. There is no redemption or salvation through any other being or source except for Jesus Christ and Him crucified as a sacrifice for our sins. We must make sure we get the name correct because names matter.

Philippians 2:9-11, "Therefore also God highly exalted Him, and bestowed on Him the name which is above every name, that at the name of Jesus every knee should bow, of those who are in heaven, and on earth, and under the earth, and that every tongue should confess that Jesus Christ is Lord, to the glory of God the Father."

People will tell you that all gods are actually the same god just called by a different name. They will tell you that all philosophy is godly if it teaches us to love others. This is a bold face lie from Satan. Names matter!!! Start at the beginning of the Old Testament and continue throughout the New Testament and you will see that it was very important to God that you referred to Him by the correct name. Allah, Buddha, Muhammad, spirit guides, one consciousness, scientology, etc. – none of these have the power to forgive or save. You have to come through the name of Jesus Christ and Him alone. This is why John was so careful to point others to Christ- he didn't want them to believe in him, only in Christ. The Word and the Holy Spirit will ALWAYS point you to Jesus Christ and Him crucified.

Luke 3:3-22, "And he came into all the district around the Jordan, preaching a baptism of repentance for the forgiveness of sins; as it is written in the book of the words of Isaiah the prophet, 'The voice of one crying in the wilderness, make ready the way of the Lord, make His paths straight. Every ravine shall be filled up, and every mountain and hill shall be brought low; and the crooked shall become straight, and the rough roads smooth; and all flesh shall see the salvation of God.' He therefore began saying to the multitudes who were going out to be baptized by him, 'You brood of vipers, who warned you to flee from the wrath to come? Therefore bring forth fruits in keeping with repentance, and do not begin to say to yourselves, 'We have Abraham for our father,' for I say to you that God is able from these stones to raise up children to Abraham. And also the axe is already laid at the root of the trees; every tree therefore that does not bear good fruit is cut down and thrown into the fire. And the multitudes were questioning him, saying, 'Then what shall we do?' And he would answer and say to them, 'Let the man who has two tunics share with him who has none; and let him who has food do likewise.' And some tax-gatherers also came to be baptized, and they said to him, 'Teacher, what shall we do?' And he said to them, 'Collect no more than what you have been ordered to.' And some soldiers were questioning him, saying, 'And what about us, what shall we do?' And he said to them, 'Do not take money from anyone by force, or accuse anyone falsely, and be content with your wages.' Now while the people were in a state of expectation and all were wondering in their hearts about John, as to whether he might be the Christ, John answered and said to them all, 'As for me, I baptize you with water; but One is coming who is mightier than I, and I am not fit to untie the thong of His sandals; He will baptize you with the Holy Spirit and fire. And His winnowing fork is in His hand to thoroughly clear His threshing floor, and to gather the wheat into His barn; but He will burn up the chaff with unquenchable fire.' So with many other exhortations also he preached the gospel to the people. But when Herod the tetrarch was reproved by him on account of Herodias, his brother's wife, and on account of all the wicked things which Herod had done, he added this also to them all, that he locked John up in prison. Now it came about when all the people were baptized, that Jesus also was baptized and while He was praying, heaven was opened and the Holy Spirit descended upon Him in bodily form like a dove and a voice came out of heaven, 'Thou are My beloved Son, in Thee I am well-pleased.'"

Look carefully at what John did to those who came out to him. He showed them their sin and told them what change needed to occur. First, he condemned those who came from the synagogues and called them a brood of vipers. He told them to bring forth fruit in accordance with repentance. He was telling them that if they had truly repented, there would be some different action on their parts taking place. But John knew there was no true repentance taking place in their hearts. He told them not to count on their heritage to save them. It doesn't matter who your parents or grandparents were. That relationship cannot save you. You have to come on your own to God. He told the tax gathers to collect only the amount that they were supposed to collect. It was common practice in that day for tax collectors to collect more than was required and to keep it for themselves. They all did it. John said that it didn't matter if everyone else was doing it, it was wrong and to truly repent, they must change their actions. He told the soldiers not to use brute force to take money or to lie about someone doing something. Again, this was common practice. All the soldiers abused their position of authority. John said that it didn't matter if everyone else was doing it, it was wrong and they had to change their actions to be truly repentant. He even told King Herod that he was wrong for committing incest and adultery. That statement got John thrown into prison but he was simply telling the truth of God and he didn't hold back even when facing a king. God says to us today, it doesn't matter if everyone around you is doing whatever you are questioning. If God revealed it to you as sin, then you must have a changed action in order to be truly repentant. If "everyone" else is reading those books, but God says it is not bringing Him glory, then you cannot read those books. If "everyone" else is watching those movies, but God has shown you that it is sin, then you cannot watch those movies. If "everyone" else is listening to that music, but God is revealing to you that it is wrong, then you cannot listen to that music. You will stand alone before God one day to answer for all that you do. "Everyone" else will not be standing there with you and God doesn't accept excuses of any kind. You choose what you will watch, read, listen to, participate in, turn away from or give in to. To be repentant and want to receive redemption and forgiveness, then there will be a change on your part.

James 4:4, "You adulteresses, do you not know that friendship with the world is hostility toward God? Therefore whoever wishes to be a friend of the world makes himself an enemy of God."

This is a powerful statement and maybe we need to post it in clear view to read every day. IF we choose to be a friend of the world and walk in the ways of the world and be accepted and do what everyone else is doing, THEN we become an enemy to God. Repentance means turning away from the ways of the world and turning completely toward God through Jesus Christ.

Ephesians 3:14-19, "For this reason, I bow my knees before the Father, from whom every family in heaven and on earth derives its name, that He would grant you, according to the riches of His glory, to be strengthened with power through His Spirit in the inner man; so that Christ may dwell in your hearts through faith; and that you, being rooted and grounded in love, may be able to comprehend will all the saints what is the breadth and length and height and depth, and to know the love of Christ which surpasses knowledge, that you may be filled up to all the fullness of God."

Confess your sins to God, be repentant and ask for His forgiveness, then receive the power of the Holy Spirit and let your life show what God can do when we walk in the fullness of Him.

John 14:27, "Peace I leave with you; My peace I give to you; not as the world gives, do I give to you. Let not your heart be troubled, nor let it be fearful."

Last thought – make sure you go to the **Word** to find forgiveness and peace. The world cannot give you the peace and power and strength and forgiveness that comes only through the Word and through the Holy Spirit living in you.

The only way to have perfect peace, is to first have the Holy Spirit living in you through your faith in Jesus Christ and your acceptance of Him as your perfect sacrifice on an old rugged cross and through your obedience of giving your life completely to Jesus Christ as Lord of your life.

If you are searching for salvation or you are just unsure of your salvation, I encourage you to contact a local pastor of a Bible-believing church and seek counseling through him. If you don't have a local church that you are comfortable with, then send me a message and let me guide you into truth of the WORD so you can find salvation or the assurance of your salvation in Jesus Christ and Christ alone.

CHAPTER FOUR

Diving into the Word

Matthew 12:42-45, "The Queen of the South shall rise up with this generation at the judgment and shall condemn it, because she came from the ends of the earth to hear the wisdom of Solomon; and behold, something greater than Solomon is here. Now when the unclean spirit goes out of a man, it passes through waterless places, seeking rest, and does not find it. Then it says, 'I will return to my house from which I came' and when it comes it finds it unoccupied, swept, and put in order. Then it goes, and takes along with it seven other spirits more wicked than itself, and they go in and live there; and the last state of that man becomes worse than the first. That is the way it will also be with this evil generation."

When we have gone through repentance and a cleansing of the heart, we need to make sure that we fill it with all of God through the study of His Word. If we want to have the fullness of God and not allow Satan and his demons the room to again take up space, we must make sure that we are actively putting more and more of God in our hearts and minds.

John 16:13, "But when He, the Spirit of truth, comes, He will guide you into all the truth; for He will not speak on His own initiative, but whatever He hears, He will speak; and He will disclose to you what is to come."

John 17:17, "Sanctify them in truth; Thy word is truth."

PRAYER – Lord God, our precious Father who gives us redemption and the forgiveness from our sins, You are holy and worthy of our praise. Father, God, You alone have the power to forgive and save us from our sins. Please Father, accept our repentance and help us to continue on this journey and find more peace through the study of Your Word. Your Word is TRUTH and we need the Holy Spirit to teach us all truth and wisdom so that we can be filled with all of You and Your Peace and Love and Joy and leave no room for satan to enter. Help us today to understand Your Word and fill us Lord. Amen and Amen

Wisdom – what is it? Do you have it? Do you have the kind that only God reveals?

Wisdom is defined through the New Oxford American Dictionary as:

The quality of having experience, knowledge and good judgment; the quality of being wise

Wise is – having or showing experience, knowledge and good judgment.

To be wise to – is to be alert to – to be aware of

Let's take a couple of quizzes and see how wise we are. First, we are going to take a US Government quiz. If we are citizens of the United States, then there are some basic things about our government that we should know. Don't cheat and look at the answers until you have completed the quiz to the best of your ability.

U.S. Government Quiz

1. How many branches of government are there according to the US Constitution?

2. How many official departments are under the executive branch? Name 5 of them.

3. What does the Secretary of State do?

4. In what article of the Constitution does it state that there must be a separation of church and state?

5. How are your Social Security investments being secured?

6. True or False: All states are required to withhold state income tax from paychecks.

7. How many senators does Mississippi have or how many does your state have?

8. How many representatives does Mississippi have or how many does your state have?

9. Which state has the most representatives? How many?

10. How many states only have 1 representative? Which one(s)?

11. How many representatives can serve by law in the house?

Answers to US Government Quiz

1. Three
2. Fifteen – Agriculture, Commerce, Defense, Education, Energy, Health & Human Services, Homeland Security, Housing & Urban Development, Justice, Labor, State, Interior, Treasury, Transportation, Veterans' Affairs
3. Manage foreign affairs
4. It is not stated in the Constitution.
5. They are not. What you pay in is being paid out to current recipients.
6. False
7. Two for Mississippi
8. Four for Mississippi
9. California – 53 (TX – 36, NY – 27, FL – 27)
10. Wyoming, US Virgin Island, Vermont, South Dakota, Puerto Rico, Northern Mariana Islands, North Dakota, Montana, Guam, DC, Delaware, American Somoa, Alaska
11. 435

Now let's see how you do with a basic Bible quiz. Again, don't cheat. Try to answer the questions before you look at the answers.

Bible Quiz

1. Where is Jesus first specifically mentioned in the Bible?

2. In what story was being sold into slavery a great blessing from God?

3. Who pouted under a tree after God exercised great forgiveness and grace to an entire city?

4. How is the Biblical blessings of Abraham related to politics today?

5. Which king lost his mind and grazed in the field like a cow for seven years?

6. What Old Testament prophet told, with specific details, of the yet to come 2nd coming of Christ to earth?

7. What will Jesus do at His next appearing to His children?

8. Which prophet was told to cut off his hair and beard; weigh the hair; divide it into thirds; burn 1/3; take 1/3 and cut it with a sword and scatter it all around town; and then take the last 1/3 and scatter it in the wind?

9. What was in the Ark of the Covenant?

10. Why did Pharaoh refuse to let the children of Israel go when Moses told him to do so?

11. Compare Passover to Salvation.

12. Name one of the two men in the Bible who never died.

13. How old is the Earth?

14. What is the only commandment with a promise?

Bible Quiz Answers

1. Genesis 3:15
2. Joseph being sold into slavery by his brothers
3. Jonah
4. God promised that whoever blessed him would be blessed and whoever cursed him would be cursed. If we bless Israel today, we will be under the blessings of God but if we curse Israel today, we will be under the curse of God.
5. King Nebuchadnezzar
6. Daniel
7. Take them to glory with Him
8. Ezekiel
9. Manna from the wilderness, Aaron's rod that budded, and the tablets of the Ten commandments
10. Because God hardened his heart
11. During the first Passover, God told the Israelites to paint the doorposts of their homes with blood from a sacrificial animal and when the death angel saw the blood he would pass over. When we are covered under the blood of Christ, Satan cannot take our lives because we are covered by God.
12. Enoch and Elijah
13. Between 5,000 and 7,000 years
14. Honor thy mother and father, that you may have long days upon this earth.

Sooooooo, how did you do? Do you feel 'not very wise' right now? That is a great starting point for all of us. We need to understand that we NEED to seek wisdom. It is ours for the taking but we must study our Bible, not just read it, as in a verse a day or once a week to be ready for a Sunday School lesson. We will need to delve into the study of the Word every single day.

Wisdom is considered by some to be simply the act of learning how to succeed in life – success and happiness come from living a life in accordance with orderliness as Proverbs 22:17 through 24:22 describes. Let's look at some selections from this passage and from Joshua.

Proverbs 22:17-21, "Incline your ear and hear the words of the wise, and apply your mind to my knowledge; for it will be pleasant if you keep them within you, that they may be ready on your lips. So that your trust may be in the Lord, I have taught you today, even you. Have I not written to you excellent things of counsels and knowledge, to make you know the certainty of the words of truth that you may correctly answer to him who sent you?"

We must not only hear wisdom from the Word but we must apply it and have it on our lips so that we are prepared to handle anything that comes our way in accordance with the truth of the WORD. If I am told that financial ruin is coming to America and I start allowing fear to paralyze me, then I will not be effective for God and I will NOT have peace. However, if I have read the WORD and KNOW that God will take care of me no matter what disasters might come, then I can have peace through wisdom even as the storm clouds gather in the distance.

Proverbs 24:13-14, "My son eat honey, for it is good, yes, the honey from the comb is sweet to your taste; know that wisdom is thus to your soul; if you find it, then there will be a future, and your hope will not be cut off."

If I have read and taken in the TRUTHs that are in the Word of God, then I have nothing to fear in my future whether it is tomorrow or ten years from now. I know how my story will end and it will be in glory worshipping at the feet of Jesus Christ my Savior. Nothing could give me more hope than that and hope will give me peace.

Joshua 1:8, "This book of law shall not depart from your mouth, but you shall meditate on it day and night, so that you may be careful to do according to all that is written in it; for then you will make your way prosperous, and then you will have success."

When we meditate – not look at – not read a verse a day – not just listen to a sermon every Sunday – really MEDITATE on the Word both day and night, THEN He will make our way prosperous. It is imperative that we act first. It is our obligation to a Holy God to determine to put His Word first and to STUDY it if we want to find wisdom that will lead to true peace in our everyday lives.

Wisdom is considered by some to be a philosophical study of the essence of life as given through Job and Ecclesiastes. We can sit and spout off a lot of philosophy about wisdom and the essence of human life but I believe God wants us to get real and know that we can have wisdom in our everyday lives that undeniably brings us power and peace.

Though the other definitions might include this, it seems that the real essence of wisdom is spiritual, for life is more than just living by a set of rules and being rewarded in some physical manner. WISDOM COMES FROM GOD!!!

Proverbs 2:6, "For the Lord gives wisdom; from His mouth come knowledge and understanding."

Proverbs 1:7, "The fear of the Lord is the beginning of knowledge; fools despise wisdom and instruction."

Malachi 2:5-6, "My covenant with him was one of life and peace, and I gave them to him as an object of reverence; so he revered Me, and stood in awe of My name. **True instruction** *was in his mouth, and unrighteousness was not found on his lips;* **he walked with Me in peace and uprightness**, *and he turned many back from iniquity."*

Peace came in knowing truth of the Word and submission to a Holy God. Revering and standing in awe is only possible when you KNOW His truth and you fully understand who God is which begins with knowledge of the Word.

Proverbs 3:13-18, **"How blessed is the man who finds wisdom, and the man who gains understanding.** *For its profit is* *better than the profit of silver, and its gain than fine gold. She (wisdom) is more precious than jewels; and nothing you desire compares with her. Long life is in her right hand; in her left hand are riches and honor. Her ways are pleasant ways, and all her paths are peace. She is a tree of life to those who take hold of her, and happy are all who hold her fast."*

When we walk in wisdom, we walk in pleasant ways and we walk a path of peace. It is worth our time to study and to learn and to seek the wisdom of God. Let's remember that knowledge and wisdom are different. Knowledge is the first step to wisdom but is not the only thing we need. Knowledge comes from reading the Bible. We study the words and we get the facts of the passage we are reading. Wisdom only comes when we stop and pray and ask the Holy Spirit to lead us into the truth of what is written. For example, it would be like reading the story of the tortoise and the hare and saying well that was interesting how the tortoise beat the hare. That would be 'to know of' the story. But wisdom comes from understanding the moral of the story that slow and steady work always brings success. Let's take the word KNOW and realize the difference in 'to know of' something or someone and 'to KNOW' someone or something. The Hebrew word for knowledge is *da'ath* which is defined as "knowing by experience, relationship or emotion." The Greek word for knowledge is *gnosis* which is defined as a deeper and better Christian knowledge both theoretical and experiential. I can say that I know Barack Obama, Johnny Cash, Billy Graham, Lady Gaga, Adolph Hitler, Celine Dion, Charles Stanley, Faith Hill, or Clint Eastwood but what I would really be saying is that I know of them – I know their names, I know their position, I know a few things about them. However, I can say that I KNOW Gary Fortenberry. I know the thoughts behind his eyes. I know what foods he will and will not eat. I know when his blood pressure is high without him saying a word. I know when he is worried and when he is mad even if his outward emotions appear the same. I know where he likes to travel and where he does not. I know what makes him uncomfortable and what brings him peace. I KNOW him because I have spent more than 37 years experiencing the ups and downs and good and bad of life with him. I don't want to know of God – I want to KNOW Him. It takes time – everyday – devoted time, walking through the valleys and on the mountaintops.

WISDOM
Takes work and
effort
but leads to the
Glory of God

Proverbs 3:1, 2, 10, 16
Ecclesiastes 10:10
Proverbs 4:18
Proverbs 2:11-12
Proverbs 2:16
Proverbs 7:1-5

FOLLY

an easy slide into

Proverbs 5:23
Proverbs 9:13-18
Proverbs 7:22
Proverbs 14:12
Proverbs 24:30-31

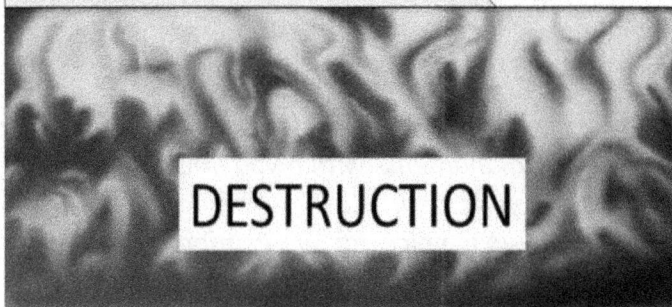

DESTRUCTION

Be sure to take time to read each of the passages listed in this design. It will help with your understanding between wisdom and folly.

*Colossians 1:9-14, "For this reason also, since the day we heard of it, we have not ceased **to pray for you and to ask that you may be filled with the knowledge of His will in all spiritual wisdom and understanding,** so that you may walk in a manner worthy of the Lord, to please Him in all respects, bearing good fruit in every good work and increasing in the knowledge of God; strengthened with all power, according to His glorious might for the attaining of all steadfastness and patience; joyously giving thanks to the Father, who has qualified us to share in the inheritance of the saints in light. For He delivered us from the domain of darkness, and transferred us to the kingdom of His beloved Son, in whom we have redemption, the forgiveness of sins."*

Start with prayer and ask that you may be filled with the knowledge of HIS will in all spiritual wisdom and understanding so that you can walk in a manner worthy of the Lord. Your being able to walk in a manner worthy of the Lord totally depends upon your knowledge that is given to you through the Holy Spirit as you study the Word of God.

*Proverbs 2:1-22, "My son, if you will receive my sayings, and treasure my commandments within you, make your ear attentive to wisdom, incline your heart to understanding; for if you cry for discernment, lift your voice for understanding; if you **seek** her as sliver, and **search** for her as for hidden treasures; then you will discern the fear of the Lord, and **discover** the knowledge of God. For the Lord gives wisdom; from His mouth come knowledge and understanding. He stores up sound wisdom for the upright; He is a shield to those who **walk** in integrity, **guarding the paths** of justice, and He **preserves the way** of His godly ones. Then you will discern righteousness and justice and equity and every good course. For wisdom will enter your heart, and knowledge will be pleasant to your soul; discretion will guard you, understanding will watch over* *you, to deliver you from the way of evil, from the man who speaks perverse things; from those who leave the paths of uprightness, to walk in the ways of darkness; who delight in doing evil, and rejoice in the perversity of evil; whose paths are crooked and who are devious in their ways; to deliver you from the strange woman, from the adulteress who flatters with her words; that leaves the companion of her youth, and forgets the covenant of her God; for the house sinks down to death, and her tracks lead to the dead; none who go to her return again, nor do they reach the paths of life. So you will **walk in the way** of good men, and **keep to the paths** of the righteous. For the upright will live in the land, and the blameless will remain in it; but the wicked will be cut off from the land, and the treacherous will be uprooted from it."*

As we learned from the definitions of wisdom and knowledge it is about experience and relationship. Experiences take time and gaining wisdom is a journey. It is not a one time reading of a book and understanding all that it can teach. It is walking in the way of the Word and gaining more knowledge and understanding as you travel down the road. You may read the same passage several times and draw deeper meaning each time that you read it. As you mature in your faith, you will better understand the depth of knowledge offered in the WORD.

Let's use the example of drinking water again here. I first learn that I need to drink water every day so that my body is not dehydrated. If I want to study further, I can learn that all water/liquids are not the same. Chemically cleaned water and bottled water still have chemical residue in the water which is not good for your body. Plastic bottled water that is left in hot vehicles releases toxins from the plastic into the water which is harmful to the body. That increases my knowledge about water and which water I should drink. You can further study to understand how water works on the cellular level in your body and just by drinking enough purified water you can heal your body of many things including many migraine headaches. I am now becoming wiser in the need that my body has for water and the correct amounts and kinds of water to drink so that I get the most benefit for my body.

The way we learn is through small bites at a time. We start with foundational knowledge and building blocks. To get off the foundation, it is necessary for you to keep going back for more information and as you learn to use the knowledge that you already have, then the next step of knowledge makes more sense.

Let's look at another example of building knowledge to get to wisdom. Think about learning to read. When you are a preschooler and you learn to draw scribbles, your parents probably praised your work and said it looked like a cat or a dog and you used your imagination as best as you could to try to see an animal. Then they began to tell you that if you drew a circle and a short line beside it that it was an "a" and that it said /a/ as in cat. Then they told you that if you made the stick longer it was a "d" and that it said /d/ as in dog. Then they turned it around and told you that it was a "b" and it said /b/ as in bird. It took you a while to figure out how to make each of those lines and understand they each had a name and a sound and some of them had more than one sound. But you finally mastered learning all the letters and then they told you if you put some of those letters together, you would have a word. From learning words, you began putting sentences together and then you were able to read paragraphs. When you learned to read, you didn't start with an applied physics text book with words that would make no sense but when you used stepping blocks you got to the point where you could at least look up those unknown words and begin to understand them. As you learned to read and read, "the stove is hot" and then you applied that knowledge to experience and discovered that when you touch a burner that is turned on, it really is hot. Knowledge plus experience gave you wisdom and you didn't touch the burner again.

That is how it is with gaining wisdom in God and therefore having peace because you understand the Word. The prerequisite to wisdom is to start with basic knowledge of God and creation and the historical accounts of Abraham and Noah and Jacob and Joseph and David and Jesus. Then you begin to understand that all the accounts go together to tell one story and then you learn that every time you read a "story" there is the actual historical account and then there is the "Living Word" which speaks to you in your time of need and gives you the instruction that you need for the day. If we stop at knowing the basic "stories" of the Bible, it would be the same as a preschooler only learning the letters and their sounds. What good did that do anyone? A person who only knew their letters and sounds would not be able to function in this world. A person who only knows Bible "stories" cannot function in this world because you will be deceived at every turn by the father of lies who knows how to manipulate and twist the stories in the Bible. You must keep learning and studying and experiencing the "Living Word of God". When you have more knowledge and experience, it is harder to be deceived; when it is harder to be deceived, there is more peace in your life.

Before we finish with wisdom bringing peace, let's address what we are to do when we have the wrong knowledge and are trying to build upon lies and half-truths which are the same as lies. Let's consider that you grew up near a beautiful serene lake. The water from late spring to early autumn was always warm near the edges and cooler toward the middle. The water was so clear that you could see fish swimming to the edge as they were feeding. You loved to go wade out in the water and feel the mud between your toes and swim peacefully in the lake for hours. Sometimes after a hard rain, the water would be muddy but it was still fun to go wading out into the water. This knowledge and experience told you that the lake was safe and secure and brought you feelings of peacefulness even when you simply thought about it. Later in life, you went on vacation to a cabin and on the far end of the property there was a beautiful lake. However, there were warning signs that said do not go into the lake because it is dangerous. But you refer to your past knowledge and experience with a lake and decide that the lake is beautiful and that to wade out into the water will bring you back to that peaceful time of childhood. So, you depend upon the knowledge that you have and you wade out into the lake but as soon as you get ankle deep you have a strange sensation on your skin. However, you ignore it and continue wading but the sensation grows and begins to be painful. Your memory is still telling you it is safe but your nerves in your skin are confirming the danger signs. You need to make a decision immediately! Do you believe your knowledge and experience from the past or do you realize that someone gave you false information or not the complete truth about lakes and change your knowledge and actions? You see, some lakes near volcanoes or near hot springs can have dangerous amounts of sulfur or acids in them. If you had never read about all types of lakes you would have been basing your knowledge on incomplete information.

So, how does this apply to our knowledge of God? If you base your knowledge on what someone has told you, for one thing, you can never be sure if they are telling the absolute truth, even if they are a well-respected person. Also, if they are only reading one verse of scripture and teaching an entire lesson on one verse, then you are not gaining the whole counsel of the Word. I will give you two examples from my personal experience. First, I was raised from the time I was conceived in a Southern Baptist Church and I was indoctrinated with Southern Baptist Theology. One of the things I was taught very well was the fact that "Christians" did NOT dance!!!!! This was drilled into my thought process and I was taught to believe that dancing was most evil. However, when I became an adult and God finally taught me that I should be studying the Word for myself, I discovered 2 Samuel 6 where the story is told of David dancing as the Ark of the Covenant was brought into Jerusalem and God didn't strike David down for dancing in joy before Him. Then I read through the Psalms where multiple times David writes about praising the Lord and letting go of our emotions and dancing before Him in the purest joy and praise. I had to change the knowledge that had been taught me all my life and know that it is OK to raise your hands and dance around and worship the Lord who gives us joy and happiness. It is even OK for us to "shout for joy"!!! We should be excited about our God who loves us and willingly gives us mercy and grace.

The second example that I will give you is how easily it is to misinterpret the scripture or to mislead someone through one single verse or a couple of verses. When I teach parenting classes, I use Deuteronomy 21:18-21 as an example of reading just one small selection of Scripture. It reads, *"If any man has a stubborn and rebellious son who will not obey his father or his mother, and when they chastise him, he will not even listen to them, then his father and mother shall seize him, and bring him out to the elders of his city at the gateway of his home town. And they shall say to the elders of his city, 'This son of ours is stubborn and rebellious, he will not obey us, he is a glutton and a drunkard,' Then all the men of his city shall stone him to death; so you shall remove the evil from your midst, and all Israel shall hear of it and fear."* We have a lot of rebellious children today and a lot of children who do not obey when they are reprimanded. So according to this word, let's take them to the elders and have them stoned to death. A little harsh isn't it?!?! You should go much deeper in this section of scriptures and see that this is intended for an extreme behavioral problem with a child. The belief behind it is that anarchy in the home breeds anarchy in society. But if we take the whole counsel of the Word and go to Proverbs 13:24, *"He who spares his rod hates his son, but he who loves him disciplines him diligently."* This passage tells us that if we love our children we will discipline them, even spanking them, to make them a better person but it does not tell us to stone them to death. So, we need to make sure that we study the whole counsel of the Word in order to understand the truth of all passages.

Understanding all of this, beware of where your knowledge and experience lead you and make sure that you have studied the

Word and the whole counsel of the Word before you set your beliefs.

Hebrews 5: 11-14, "Concerning him we have much to say, and it is hard to explain, since you have become dull of hearing. For though by this time you ought to be teachers, you have need again for someone to teach you the elementary principles of the oracles of God, and you have come to need milk and not solid food. For everyone who partakes only of milk is not accustomed to the word of righteousness, for his is a babe. But solid food is for the mature, who because of practice have their senses trained to discern good and evil."

Elementary knowledge and building blocks are necessary to gain knowledge that leads to wisdom, BUT we cannot stay there. It is imperative that we keep going back to study more and to apply it to more experiences so that we can truly gain wisdom and become mature Christians who are able to discern good and evil in this world that is so very deceptive.

*Proverbs 8:22-36, "The Lord possessed me (wisdom) at the beginning of His way, before His works of old. From everlasting I was established, from the beginning, from the earliest times of the earth. When there were no depths I was brought forth, when there were no springs abounding with water. Before the mountains were settled, before the hills I was brought forth; while He had not yet made the earth and the fields, nor the first dust of the world. When He established the heavens, I was there, when He inscribed a circle on the face of the deep, when He made firm the skies above, when the springs of the deep became fixed, when He set for the sea its boundary, so that the water should not transgress His command, when He marked out the foundations of the earth; then I was beside Him, as a master workman; and I was daily His delight, rejoicing always before Him, rejoicing in the world, His earth, and having my delight in the sons of men. **Now, therefore, O sons, listen to me, for blessed are they who keep my ways. Heed instruction and be wise, and do not neglect it. Blessed is the man who listens to me,*** *watching daily at my gates, waiting at my doorposts.* **For he who finds me finds life, and obtains favor from the LORD.** **But he who sins against me injures himself; all those who hate me love death**."

We must sit daily at the gates of wisdom and heed instruction in order to find life. The gateway to wisdom is found in the Bible, in the whole counsel of the Word.

John 1:1-5, 14-18, "*In the beginning was the Word, and the Word was with God, and the Word was God. He was in the beginning with God. All things came into being by Him, and apart from Him nothing came into being that has come into being. In Him was life, and the life was the light of men. And the light shines in the darkness, and the darkness did not comprehend it....*

And the Word became flesh and dwelt among us and we beheld His glory, glory as of the only begotten from the Father, full of grace and truth. John bore witness of Him, and cried out, saying, 'This was He of whom I said, 'He who comes after me has a higher rank than I, for He existed before me.'' For of His fullness we have all received, and grace upon grace. For the Law was given through Moses; **grace and truth were realized through Jesus Christ.** *No man has seen God at any time;* **the only begotten God, who is in the bosom of the Father, He has explained Him.**"

How do we understand all the Bible has to offer? We start with Jesus who was the Word that became flesh and dwelt among us to explain God to us. Start by reading the gospels of Matthew, Mark, Luke and John. Learn from the teachings of Jesus to gain the knowledge to begin your journey toward wisdom which will lead you into peace.

Colossians 2:1-3, "*For I want you to know how great a struggle I have on your behalf, and for those who are at Laodicea, and for all those who have not personally seen my face, that their hearts may be encouraged, having been knit together in love, and attaining to all the wealth that comes from the full assurance of understanding, resulting in a true knowledge of God's mystery, that* is, Christ Himself, in whom are hidden all the treasures of wisdom and knowledge."

Our treasure that we are to search for is found in Christ Jesus Himself. Search for knowledge there and apply His teachings and then you will gain experience and wisdom will follow and strengthen you.

But BEWARE – for as you study, the craftiness of Satan will enter in and try to mislead you and take you to materials where the Bible is referenced and then distorted. Heed the instruction and wisdom for the following passages.

Luke 11:49-52, "For this reason also, the wisdom of God said, 'I will send to them prophets and apostles, and some of them they will kill and some they will persecute, in order that the blood of all the prophets , shed since the foundation of the world, may be charged against this generation, from the blood of Abel to the blood of Zechariah, who perished between the altar and the house of God; yes, I tell you, it shall be charged against this generation.' Woe to you lawyers! For you have taken away the keys of knowledge; you did not enter in yourselves, and those who were entering in you hindered."

Matthew 24:24, "For false Christs and false prophets will arise and will show great signs and wonders, so as to mislead, if possible, even the elect."

*Mark adds this in chapter 13:21-23, "And then if anyone says to you, 'Behold, here is the Christ'; or 'behold, He is there'; do not believe him; for false Christs and false prophets will arise, and show signs and wonders, in order, if possible, to lead the elect astray. **But take heed; behold I have told you everything in advance**."*

John 16:33, "These things I have spoken to you, that in Me you may has peace. In the world you have tribulation, but take courage; I have overcome the world."

God says that MANY false prophets and teachers will come and try to mislead the elect and the chosen ones. But He reminds us that if we are studying His Word and listening to His teachings, then we will not be deceived. So how do we determine if teachings are true or false? First, you must know the WORD and be able to go back to the references made and determine if it was written as it was stated by the teacher. Don't let the teaching start in the middle of a sentence. Go back to what was said in the reference prior to the given verse and read further beyond what was said in the verse. Then cross reference the material to see what else the Bible says about that subject. Second, speak to others who you have come to trust, and weigh their thoughts against the item taught and what you have read in Scripture. Praying through this the Holy Spirit will bring you to the divine wisdom of the Scripture. You DO NOT have to have a theology degree so understand the Scriptures. The Holy Spirit is our teacher who brings all knowledge and understanding to us. Next, consider the teaching, in light of the following passage.

James 3:13-18, *"Who among you is wise and understanding? Let him show by his good behavior his deeds in the gentleness of wisdom. But if you have bitter jealousy and selfish ambition in your heart, do not be arrogant and so lie against the truth. This wisdom is not that which comes down from above, but is earthly, natural, demonic. For where jealousy and selfish ambition exists, there is disorder and every evil thing. But the wisdom from above is first **PURE**, then **PEACABLE**, **GENTLE**, **REASONABLE**, **FULL OF MERCY** and **GOOD FRUITS**, **UNWAVERING**, **WITHOUT HYPOCRISY**. And the seed whose fruit is righteousness is **SOWN IN PEACE** by those who make peace."*

It is my prayer that the Holy Spirit will guide you through this lesson and set the Word in your mind and heart so that you can recall it when you are faced with life events and that you will keep going back to the Word daily to gain more and more knowledge.

Then as you apply the Word and heed the instruction you will gain experience which will lead to wisdom and wisdom will lead to the peace of God.

CHAPTER FIVE

Communicating with Jehovah

The only One who has the power to change our circumstances or change us in our circumstances is way too often the last One we communicate with about our circumstances.

1 Thessalonians 5:16-19, "Rejoice always; pray without ceasing; in everything give thanks; for this is God's will for you in Christ Jesus."

James 5:13-18, "Is anyone among you suffering? Then he must pray. Is anyone cheerful? He is to sing praises. Is anyone among you sick? Then he must call for the elders of the church and they are to pray over him, anointing him with oil in the name of the Lord; and the prayer offered in faith will restore the one who is sick, and the Lord will raise him up, and if he has committed sins, they will be forgiven him. Therefore, confess your sins to one another, and pray for one another so that you may be healed. The effective prayer of a righteous man can accomplish much. Elijah was a man with a nature like ours, and he prayed earnestly that it would not rain, and it did not rain on the earth for three years and six months. Then he prayed again, and the sky poured rain and the earth produced its fruit."

Oh, Father God, Jehovah, when will we ever learn to fall at your feet continually so that we have the strength and wisdom and power to effectively live life in perfect peace. Oh, Precious Lord, help us to not just know but to internalize the wisdom that comes from praying without ceasing. Teach us Dear Lord what that means and how to reorganize our lives so that we do this as our first response and not our desperate last call. You and You alone are all-powerful and all-knowing and all-present and You alone can change our circumstances or change us in our circumstances. Give each of us the desire in our hearts to want to come to You before we even breathe a word to anyone else. Father, help us to understand communication not just with our words that we want to hear but with our hearts that You want to hear. Remind us that communication is a two-way street and we need to be willing to listen to You through Your Word and through Your Holy Spirit as You speak to our spirit. Help us to be still so that we can hear Your still small voice above the shouts and screams and noise of this world. Amen and Amen!

In 1 Thessalonians, Paul tells us that we should pray without ceasing and rejoice always. We have already covered how we can rejoice in the midst of trials and tribulations but how do we pray without ceasing. First, we should understand that communication with God is not just about sitting down with our eyes closed and our hands folded in some special "prayer" position. We are far inferior to a most Holy and Superior God and so our prayers must be with a most holy and awe-inspired fear and respect. However, within that realm of respect, God wants to hear from us and hear from us often. The entire purpose of our creation was to communicate our love towards our Creator. He created us to talk to Him. Since that is the summation of our purpose, shouldn't we make that a daily, maybe hourly, maybe constant, priority? We also must recognize that there is NO magic formula to prayer.

Matthew 6:7-8, "And when you are praying, do not use meaningless repetition as the Gentiles do, for they suppose that they will be heard for their many words. So do not be like them; for your Father knows what you need before you ask Him."

Jesus, Himself, taught that we are not to use meaningless words or repetitive words. We teach our kids to pray poems because we think it is cute to hear them say a repeated blessing or a repeated nighttime prayer but is that really teaching them to talk to God? Do you teach them repetitive things to say to their grandparents every time they see them? God doesn't want to hear what someone else wrote, He wants to hear your heart and your words that come from your heart. He wants to hear when you are angry or hurt or happy. He already KNOWS how your heart feels so be honest and tell Him. Don't fear communication with God because you think you don't know how to pray. I often use this story to teach my high school students about real, every day, honest communication with God. When I was a young mother, my own mother had had knee surgery and was in a hospital about an hour away from our home. They day after her surgery, I had a meeting at church which required that I be in a dress and heels. After my meeting, I went and picked up our daughter who was around two years of age at that time. We were in my husband's truck and we had to go to my parents' farm to pick up some personal items that my mother needed and then we were going to drive to the hospital to see her. When I drove up to the farm, I saw that a cow had gotten out of the pasture and was in the yard. So, my thoughts started racing – if I neglected the cow and it got out to the highway and someone had an accident because of the cow they could sue my parents and I didn't want that to happen to them, nor did I want them to lose the cow as the farm was part of their income. My dad was out of town at work and it was in the middle of the day so all the neighbors were at work also. I reasoned that if I gently tried to guide her through an open gate to the lot beside the yard, she could stay safely in there until my dad got home to put her back in the pasture. That should be easy enough since she was normally such an easy and slow cow. I rolled down the window in the truck and left my daughter in there so she would be out of the way. I started walking toward the cow in my dress and heels and start motioning at her to turn around and move through the gate. Well, the dog got excited when I started motioning for the cow to move and the dog decided to help. The dog's help made the cow move faster than I wanted and in the wrong direction. All the action was quite a show for my young daughter and she started jumping up and down and beating on the steering wheel which is where the horn is located. The dog was barking and chasing the cow and my daughter was beating on the horn and I was in my dress and heels. I walked as quickly as I could around the house to try to stop the cow but the dog had her going in circles. If someone had been filming the chaos, we could have won a lot of money on America's Funniest Videos. I stopped at that moment and looked up at God and just screamed, "Please help me get the cow in the gate!" I wasn't being disrespectful. I wasn't shouting out demands. I was simply crying out to the only ONE who could change my circumstances. At that instant, the dog stopped barking and the horn stopped blowing and the cow walked right through the gate and I closed it behind her. God heard and answered my prayer. No formal words, no formal actions, just a desperate cry for help to the only One who could help me. How much easier it would have been had I had that conversation with Him before I began my own determined actions.

Praying without ceasing is an attitude more than it is an action. Over the years, I have learned that I am in constant communication with God in my heart and my mind. It is a state of being that we need to learn to live in constantly. Being constantly aware of the presence of God. Being constantly aware of the source of help and comfort and peace and joy and gladness and blessings that come only from Him. Pray without ceasing.

Then James tells us that whatever is going on, PRAY. Pray with our families and our friends and our church families. Gather together to pray. Have some old-fashioned prayer meetings where you really spend time praying not gossiping or visiting. James tells us there is power in prayer and where there is power there is peace. When we turn our thoughts towards God as Creator or Comforter or Healer or Friend or Savior, we change our focus off our worries and onto His abilities. One of the most powerful things in prayer is praise. When we 'count our blessings', we focus on what we have and not what we don't have. When we praise the name of Jesus, all the power of heaven is invited into our lives and there is NO power on earth or under the earth or above the earth or in the center of the earth or in the center of your life that can stand against the power of our Almighty God.

Let's use Psalm 100 to dig into how praise can bring peace in our lives as we communicate with our Holy God, Jehovah. We will take it apart and look at each piece and make sure we don't miss one single nugget of wisdom this passage offers us.

Psalm 100:

"Shout joyfully to the Lord all the earth." If you need to force yourself to praise the LORD, then there are deeper things in your life that need to be dealt with. Notice the writer says to shout. We have no problem shouting at sporting events as we cheer on our favorite team, be that pro teams or little league teams. I can't tell you the times I have heard people hoarse from hollering at sporting events in which they had absolutely no investment in the outcome of that event, they just wanted their chosen team to win. I've watched family members jump high out of their seats and scream like a house was on fire because a four-year-old hit a ball off a tee and he ran around the bases and touched home plate. I've stood in a stadium and watched hundreds of people jump to their feet and shout with all they had as they watched a high school football player run down a grassy field with an inflated piece of leather and cross over a painted line. How much more should we be willing to SHOUT JOYFULLY to our precious LORD!! Shouting joyfully comes from a heart overflowing with joy that cannot be controlled or pushed down. If you are not able to praise from an overflowing heart, there may be things (sins, unforgiveness, anger, hurts) that must be dealt with before you can shout joyfully. Or maybe, you don't fully understand God's most precious gift of mercy and grace that He so freely offers to you, that cost Him everything but only requires your devotion and obedience and acceptance. Stop and ask God to reveal to you what is keeping you from having joy overflowing into shouts of praise. He will show you

and He will show you what to do with them, BUT you must be obedient to what He tells you if you want to cleanse your heart of what harnesses your joy and your shouting.

"Serve the Lord with gladness." Wow, this one you cannot do unless you are walking in the Spirit daily. We have self-service and self-gratification so worldly ingrained in us, that it takes power from the Holy Spirit to get self out of our way so that we can serve (AS A SERVANT) in any way God wants us to serve and then to do it with gladness. Serving is not easy in today's society. We are taught to think of self above all others and to never let anyone put us down or expect us to "wait" on them. When we were a young married couple and we would go over to my in-laws' house for a visit, at some point in each visit, my mother-in-law would always ask if anyone wanted coffee, which was always made at their house. Then all the wives would get up and go fix their husbands coffee and bring it to them. As a young, often smart aleck, young wife, I would simply look at Gary and ask him if anything was wrong with his legs because he could get up and fix his own coffee. It took God a while to work on me with that and teach me that I was being first disrespectful to my mother-in-law in that attitude but also, that I had a heart problem when it came to service. After many years, God has shown me that I can serve my husband as He teaches me to do and I will receive far greater blessings in my service than I ever would have in my self-righteous and smart aleck responses. Oh, how I thank God for a mother and a mother-in-law who taught not by words but by actions of what it was like to serve the Lord with gladness by serving others around us. Jesus gave us the example of washing one another's feet which is a very lowly serving job. If Jesus can lower Himself, the very son of God Almighty, then we can lower ourselves into a servant role and serve wherever He leads us to serve. Your act of service might not be for the world to acknowledge or for personal praise but it will be for the Father in Heaven to take notice and be able to say "well done Thy good and

faithful servant". But He wants our service to be done with gladness. How much do you tell God thanks for allowing you to serve? He could have chosen someone else to serve Him in any capacity that He wanted. However, He chose you and you should always thank Him for allowing you to be a part of His service and then serve with gladness. When you are conscience of how He uses you each day in different areas of service, then you begin to thank Him. When you begin to thank Him, you begin to serve more and more with gladness. Take some time and talk to Him about how He wants you to serve in your family or in your church or in your community or maybe even in your own family. If He leads you into an act of service that you might feel is beneath your quality, go back and ask Him to do a work in your heart and remember that He requires obedience in little things before He will ask us about bigger things. Praise Him for being able to serve in whatever place He has you because that place is important to HIM and He is the only One who matters.

"Come before Him with joyful singing." Do you sing praise songs to God? I tell everyone that is one thing I can always do Biblically because I can most certainly 'make a joyful noise'. God doesn't care about the quality of our voices. He cares about the praise that originates in our hearts and THEN flows out of our mouths. We live in an electronic age where we can pull up praise music at the touch of a finger. We don't even have to purchase it. I can sit in front of my television set and pull up YouTube videos of praise. I can do the same thing on my phone or computer. There is no place and no time that I cannot play worship music. Whatever source you use, listen to and sing along with praise music daily. Find a song with words that tell God how you want to praise Him. Music can bring so much to prayer time and worship time. It gets our hearts lined up and in tune with the heart of God. This may be an area that is robbing you of your peace that you need to deal with before you can move forward. What type of music do you listen to on a daily basis? Music feeds our soul and in the depths of our soul

is where we find our perfect peace. What are you feeding your soul??? I had a young mother tell me one time that she was trying to listen to more country music instead of the hard rock that she normally listened to each day. She was trying to get a confirmation from me that she was doing something good. Too many people, especially in the south have this mentality that country music is more 'godly'. That is a LIE! Most country songs are about infidelity and drinking and looking at someone else's spouse. That is not of GOD. It is not about the rhythm at all. It is about the words. There is also a flip side to this. There are many songs labeled and sold as "Christian" that are as false as Satan is real. It is imperative that you feed your soul with music that glorifies God and restores and strengthens your soul. Pay close attention to the words of what you are listening to on your devices. Ask God to reveal what is truth and what is stealing your peace as it stirs your soul in the wrong way.

"Know that the Lord Himself is God; It is He who has made us, and not we ourselves; We are HIS people and the sheep of His pasture." If you asked Jesus to be your LORD and Savior, then you belong to Him. We are HIS and He can do whatever He wants with our lives. He can allow us to go through whatever trial that He wants us to go through. We are His sheep and He can put us in whatever pasture He wants. He can choose to put us in a pasture where we have material things of this world or He can choose to put us in a pasture where we have very little that the world offers. I can tell you from experience that when I have all of Jesus I don't care at all about what the world offers and there is GREAT freedom there. I don't care about what anyone else has. I am not worried that I have the newest or latest edition of what I already have. I am full and satisfied when I have all of Jesus. There is sure and strong and never wavering peace there. When we recognize this, we are fully giving ourselves to Him and that is praise to Him. When I truly thank Him for what I have, then I am not wanting more of what I don't need. I trust Him to provide whatever I need to do the work

He has called me to do for HIM. If we could completely settle this in our hearts, we would be so filled with peace that everyone who met us along our journey would take notice and want what we have. Let Jesus be Lord and allow HIM to lead and guide and give and take as HE sees fit and then allow Him to use you there for HIS glory and HIS glory alone. Then nothing else matters!

"Enter His gates with thanksgiving, and His courts with praise. Give thanks to Him, bless His name." Make a list of things that you are thankful for. Keep the list going and add to it each day. It is a powerful thing to give thanks to God. Dig deep to see how many things you can put on your list of what you have been blessed with from God. Everything you have is a gift from God. If you need help here, I would point you to Ann Voskamp's book "One Thousand Gifts". When we begin to see everything we have as a blessing from God, we see Him in all of His glory and we take away Satan's power to defeat us and make us feel unworthy and neglected. Satan works so strongly through advertising and our own selfishness to convince us that we MUST have more and more and more. And God sits back and desires so strongly for us to recognize what we have and to be thankful for each and every thing. Did you wake up this morning and see the beautiful world around you? Did you thank God for your vision? Did you wake up this morning and hear the morning sounds around you? Did you thank God for your ability to hear? Did you wake up this morning and stand on your own two feet? Did you thank Him for that ability? I could go on and on and on but that is your assignment. Get out that notebook and start writing them down. Remember to dig deep and see how far you can go. I'm sure that each of us could go far beyond 1000 gifts if we tried every day. And boy oh boy would our focus ever be changed!!

"For the Lord is good; His lovingkindness is everlasting, and His faithfulness to all generations." When you stop to pray, focus on who God is and not what you want. It will change your prayer life and it will change your life altogether. Give Him the praise due

Him today. He is good and faithful. He loves you far more than you could ever love yourself. He loves you in spite of any sin you could have ever committed. He wants to bring you onto HIS path that HE prepared just for you, full of blessings that are far beyond your wildest imagination. He will never make you a puppet to do only as He wants. He gives you free will to do as you choose. But you can only receive those blessings if you get on and stay on the path HE has prepared for you. God created you. You wouldn't exist if it weren't for a loving God who chose to give you life and to sustain you in your life. But above that, He gives you the gift of eternal life. If all God ever did for me was to send His Son, Jesus Christ, to live as an example for me and to die as a sacrifice for my sins and to rise again as a living Savior, then I would already have more than enough to praise Him for every second of every minute of every hour of every day, 365 days a year. But God provides for me and cares for me each day and so I have journals upon journals of things for which I can praise Him. Walk away from all the things that rob your soul of peace and give that time to God. Give Him your complete focus and think about Him and His great love for you. The praise will come and with the praise, joy will come and with the joy, peace will come.

Let's look at some events in the Bible where God's people prayed and see how their prayers changed their circumstances or changed them in their circumstances.

Acts 2: 36-47, "Therefore let all the house of Israel know for certain that God has made Him both Lord and Christ – this Jesus whom you crucified.' Now when they heard this, they were pierced to the heart, and said to Peter and the rest of the apostles, 'Brethren, what shall we do?' And Peter said to them, 'Repent, and let each of you be baptized in the name of Jesus Christ for the forgiveness of your sins; and you shall receive the gift of the Holy Spirit. For the promise is for you and your children, and for all who are far off, as many as the Lord our God shall call to Himself.' And with many other words he solemnly testified and kept on exhorting *them, saying, "Be saved from this perverse generation!' So them, those who had received his word were baptized; and there were added that day about three thousand souls. And they were **continually devoting themselves** to the apostles' teaching and to fellowship and to the breaking of bread **and to prayer**. And **everyone kept feeling a sense of awe**; and <u>many wonders and signs were taking place</u> through the apostles. And all those who had believed were together, and had all things in common; and they began selling their property and possessions, and were sharing them with all, as anyone had need. And day by day continuing with one mind in the temple, and breaking bread from house to house, they were taking their meals together with gladness and sincerity of heart, praising God, and having favor with all the people. And the Lord was adding to their number day by day those who were saved."*

When these new believers came together they were continually - as in all the time - morning, noon and night – devoting (making a priority) to prayer and other acts of service to God. They didn't welcome each other and have an opening prayer and move on with their activities and then close in prayer before everyone went home. They were not telling a friend "I'll pray for you" and then going on about their business and never really praying for their friend. They were spending time on their knees in prayer. I imagine that they were spending hours in prayer over their friends that the friends would come to know Jesus. How much time do you really spend in prayer? Do you start your day off with a conversation with God? Do you fall to your knees when someone asks for prayer? Do you pray before you travel? Do you pray before you begin your job and ask God to use you today? God gives us this example in HIS word to show us that devoted prayer will bring results. Notice that the passage tells us that they felt a sense of awe and that many signs and wonders were taking place. God moved because the people were totally surrendered to HIM. Is your prayer life one of total devotion to God and not to your schedule? One morning as I was working on this chapter, Satan kept reminding me that I needed to go and pick blueberries instead of working on this writing because it was going to rain in the afternoon. He was reminding me that I needed that bounty of God's provision because blueberries are full of God's medicine that will help heal my body from pain. Satan is very good at what he does as he tries to deceive us. However, God said to work on HIS lessons in the morning and He would provide ample time for me to go and pick blueberries. Whatever Satan uses to try to deceive you, stand your ground and let him know that you trust God totally and will only follow after God's leading. This takes practice and failure and getting back up and doing it all over again tomorrow. God uses your failure, which He knows will come, to strengthen you and make you better prepared for the next challenge from Satan. DEVOTED CONTINUAL PRAYER – makes things happen when you are walking with God and be prepared because most often the change comes from within you not from others. If you read all the passage above, you will see that their hearts were changed and they began getting rid of what they didn't need so they could help others. Be prepared for the change to be in you and you must be ready to give all you have back to God. You will need to let go of any and all that God tells you to let go of for HIS glory.

Another thing to remember in this passage is that these people were praying and living under Roman rule. Roman rule was one of the cruelest reigns of any government. They invented and enjoyed crucifixion. They would kill you instantly for doing anything they deemed wrong whether it was law or not. These that accepted Jesus Christ as Lord and Savior did so knowing that they would become the number one enemy of the Romans who were cruel to everyone but even more so to Christians. Notice that they were taking their meals together with GLADNESS. This is important because we want to make excuses and say that no one really knows what we are going through. These early Christians were faced with cruel deaths just to say they were Christians, yet they met together for concentrated prayer and they got rid of all that they didn't need to bring God glory and they ate meals together with GLAD hearts. Prayer is powerful and can bring peace and joy and gladness in the worse possible conditions.

Acts 6:4, "But we will devote ourselves to prayer and to the ministry of the word."

Again, we see the words DEVOTE OURSELVES TO PRAYER. One thing I have learned in the past two years, as I have done my best to totally surrender everything to God and what He wants, is that I should be prepared to have interruptions and to deal with God's business at any time during the day. In devoting myself to prayer, I must be ready when someone calls or comes by or sends a message on Facebook or through text or email, to stop what I am doing and to listen to them and to pray with them right then and there. And yes, sometimes that may take as much as an hour out of my day but God's blessings through it are tremendous. Many think that since I am self-employed and that I set my own work hours and schedules that I shouldn't have any problem meeting with people and spending time with them to pray. Over the past few years, I have been a caregiver to my mother, my mother-in-law and now my husband as he battles through cancer. Being a caregiver is a difficult and time-consuming job. I take care of our house and prepare nutritional healing foods. I help with gardening and growing more nutritionally sound food for our families. I teach a group of youth, making sure they not only have a solid education in math, language, science and history, but that they also have a solid foundation on living daily with God as their guide. I write social media devotions, Bible lessons and journals as God leads. So, I do understand busy schedules BUT I know the joy and blessings that come when I set aside my schedule and pray with or for someone that God lays on my heart. It all has to do with what is a priority in our own heads and in our own hearts. If my priority is to be used of God, then nothing else matters and He rules my minutes and my days. In God's great design of teaching, I am counseling with two separate ladies through email while I am writing this lesson. I stop and pray with them as God leads me to do so. Like I said the blessing is far greater than any inconvenience that Satan might try to convince me exists. DEVOTED TO PRAYER.

Acts 12:3-11, *"And when he saw that it pleased the Jews, he proceeded to arrest Peter also. Now it was during the days of Unleavened Bread. And when he had seized him, he put him in prison, delivering him to four squads of soldiers to guard him, intending after the Passover to bring him out before the people. So Peter was kept in the prison, **but prayer for him was being made fervently by the church of God**. And on the very night when Herod was about to bring him forward, Peter was sleeping between two soldiers, bound with two chains; and guards in front of the door were watching over the prison. And behold, an angel of the Lord suddenly appeared, and a light shone in the cell; and he struck Peter's side and roused him saying, 'Get up quickly.' And his chains fell off his hands. And the angel said to him, 'Gird yourself and put on your sandals.' And he did so. And he said to him, 'Wrap your cloak around you and follow me.' And he went out and continued to follow, and he did not know that what was being done by the angel was real, but thought he was seeing a vision. And when they had passed the first and second guard, they came to the iron gate that leads into the city, which opened for them by itself; and they went out and went along one street; and immediately the angel departed from him. And when Peter came to himself, he said, '**Now I know for sure that the Lord has sent forth His angel and rescued me** from the hand of Herod and from all that the Jewish people were expecting."*

Our devoted prayers for others are important. When we devote ourselves to praying for others, their chains break and they find freedom in Christ. I see it on a regular basis as I see young people changed not because of me but because of our prayer and investment in them to continually lift them up before God and continually ask the Lord to do a mighty work in their lives. If you love your relatives and friends pray for them. Allow the Holy Spirit to prompt you to pray for others and when you feel that need to pray, stop immediately what you are doing and pray. The more you do this, the more God will bring to your spirit the need to pray for others. God has changed my thoughts and focus on this drastically in the past years. Even when I respond on social media to a prayer request from someone, I now write out my prayer for them instead of just saying that I will pray. When someone asks me to pray for them, I stop and do it right then and not just say, "OK, I will" and then walk away. When God reveals a prayer need to you, then you should be devoted to praying for that person until the circumstance is changed or the person is changed in the circumstance or until God says stop. Often we pray a quick prayer once and then move on to the next thing that piques our interest. We must learn to stop and stay in one place and dwell there for a while in prayer, while God moves in the hearts of others and in our hearts. Prayer is not a quick fix kind of place. We need to linger there for a while. If we learn to pray diligently for others, we will have a much greater appreciation for those who are our prayer warriors when we are walking through the valley. When we listen to the Holy Spirit in the small things, we will be able to hear Him better in the larger things. It is a lesson in obedience to the prompting of the Holy Spirit.

Acts 16:13-32, "And on the Sabbath day we went outside the gate to a riverside, where we were supposing that there would be a place of prayer; and we sat down and began speaking to the women who had assembled. And a certain woman named Lydia, from the city of Thyatira, a seller of purple fabrics, a worshiper of God, was listening; and the Lord opened her heart to respond to the things spoken by Paul. And when she and her household had been baptized, she urged us, saying, 'If you have judged me to be faithful to the LORD, come into my house and stay.' And she prevailed upon us. And it happened that as we were going to the place of prayer, a certain slave-girl having a spirit of divination met us, who was bringing her masters much profit by fortunetelling. Following after

*Paul and us, she kept crying out, saying, 'These men are bond-servants of the Most High God, who are proclaiming to you the way of salvation.' And she continued doing this for many days. But Paul was greatly annoyed, and turned and said to the spirit, 'I command you in the name of Jesus Christ to come out of her!' And it came out of her at that very moment. But when her masters saw that their hope of profit was gone, they seized Paul and Silas and dragged them into the market place before the authorities, and when they had brought them to the chief magistrates, they said, 'These men are throwing our city into confusion, being Jews, and are proclaiming customs which it is not lawful for us to accept or to observe , being Romans.' And the crowd rose up together against them and the chief magistrates tore their robes off them, and proceeded to order them to be beaten with rods. And when they had inflicted many blows upon them, they threw them into prison, commanding the jailer to guard them securely; and he, having received such a command, threw them into the inner prison, and fastened their feet in the stocks. **But about midnight Paul and Silas were praying and singing hymns of praise to God,** and the prisoners were listening to them; and suddenly there came a great earthquake, so that the foundations of the prison house were shaken; and **immediately all the doors were opened, and everyone's chains were unfastened**. And when the jailer had been roused out of sleep and had seen the prison doors opened, he drew his sword and was about to kill himself, supposing that the prisoners had escaped. But Paul cried out with a loud voice, saying, 'Do yourself no harm, for we are all here!' And he called for lights and rushed in and, trembling with fear, he fell down before Paul and Silas, and after he brought them out, he said, 'Sirs, what must I do to be saved?' And they said, 'Believe in the Lord Jesus, and you shall be saved, you and your household.' And they spoke the word of the Lord to him together with all who were in his house."*

In the previous passage, we saw where the prayers of others delivered Peter from the prison. However, in this passage, we see that the prayers of Paul and Silas changed the jailor and his family. Please don't miss the part of this passage that tells how Paul and Silas were treated before being thrown into prison. They were pushed around and beaten with a rod and then thrown into prison. The prisons of their day were NOTHING like the prisons that we see today. During an archeological dig in Philippi, they discovered what they believe is the prison that Paul and Silas were in during the time of the above passage. It was small and damp and totally enclosed. It is described as being like a cistern that would hold a large amount of water. It is further stated that if this is in fact the prison of Paul and Silas that the other prisoners would have had no choice but to listen to them. It was a crowded small area. They had been beaten and they were secured in stocks. Can you imagine open wounds that have not been cared for and then placed in stocks where you cannot move? I know I would NOT be happy or wanting to be singing praises but that is exactly what they did. Paul and Silas knew that God was still there and He was still caring for them but they also knew that their lives were God's to use any way that HE saw fit to bring Him glory and to bring others into HIS kingdom. So, they prayed and cried out to God and then sang praises glorifying Him for who HE was. God opened up the stocks that held them and opened up the prison doors but they were so close in communication with God and so in tune with the Holy Spirit that they knew they were not to leave but to witness. As they knew what their mission was from God and that they were to stay and not flee from the prison, many were saved. That was God's work and He used them in prison to accomplish HIS work.

As we have seen through these Biblical accounts, devoted prayer and communication with God brings you in tune with the Holy Spirit and you will know when to go and when to stay and when to speak and when to stay silent. Our fears and anger and anguish will subside at the feet of Jesus. There is no greater peace than to be in communication with God and KNOW His voice and know your place and your instructions. You can have peace in the midst of life's greatest trials when you have an open and devoted communication with God whether He removes us from those trials or walks with us through the trial, holding us ever so tightly but ever so gently. We must remember to go to HIM first and not after we have failed miserably at trying our own way. Communicating with our Creator can and will bring perfect peace into our minds and hearts and souls as He draws our focus to Him.

CHAPTER SIX

Reining in my Thoughts and Actions

In the first five chapters, we have discussed how to obtain that perfect peace that only God can give. But now we need to find out how to keep it and not become overwhelmed with life once again.

Father in heaven, thank You for Your guide book that contains all the truth we need to live a life of peace that honors and glorifies You. Thank You for plain and simple instructions that allow us to see You and to experience You and to KNOW You. When we are with others of the same mind and heart it all sounds so easy but then we walk back into our lives - it seems so hard. Help us today continue to use Your guide book to help us see what we must do to walk daily with You so that we continue in Your peace and continue bringing honor and glory to You. Help us to find others that will encourage us on our walk and hold us accountable when they see us slipping away from Your perfect path. Father, may Your Word do all the teaching and may Your Holy Spirit guide us into all TRUTH as we study these lessons together.

Where do we start? How do we live each day so that we retain this peace that we have found? We start with the greatest and most important commandment as told by Jesus.

Deuteronomy 6:4 -5 "Hear, O Israel! The Lord is our God, the Lord is one! You shall love the Lord your God with all your heart and with all your soul and with all your might."

In all that we do, it should be done because of our great love for God. Our heart should be pure so that we can worship Him in Spirit and truth. Our soul, our character, our inner core, should shout to others that Jesus is LORD and that we serve the ONE and only True God. Our might, our power, should come from HIS power that He freely gives to all of us who bow down to HIM. Do you LOVE Him or do you just want Him around every now and then when you are in trouble and need help? Do you love Him like you did your first true love? Remember how giddy you would get? Do you remember how much of your time was spent thinking about that young man (or young lady if you happen to be a man)? Do you remember how much time was spent conversing with that person? In Revelation 2:4, God tells John to write to Ephesus how He recognizes the good they have done BUT, "you have left your first love." God wants to be our first love. He wants to be our first love every minute of every day. Does your life reflect how much you love God? This is an awkward question because the truth is that your life DOES reflect how much you love God. That being true, what does your life reflect to others? Do they see you or do they see God in all of HIS glory? How do you love God with all your heart and soul and might?

Deuteronomy 6:6-9, "These words, which I am commanding you today, shall be on your heart. You shall teach them diligently to your sons and shall talk of them when you sit in your house and when you walk by the way and when you lie down and when you rise up. You shall bind them as a sign on your hand and they shall be as frontals on your forehead. You shall write them on the doorposts of your house and on your gates."

God and His Word should be ever before us. A frontal was something that hung in "front" of your eyes for you to focus on throughout the day. It would be something like a baseball cap with Scripture dangling from the bib in front of your eyes all day long. The priests became competitive with it and tried to make their frontals better than others'. Jesus had to come and explain to us dumb little sheep that it was not for others to see and judge us but for us to see to remind us to LOVE GOD MORE THAN ANYTHING ELSE!! He wanted His Word in our hands and in front of our eyes at all times, NOT for others to see how religious we might be but for us to be constantly reminded that HE and HE alone has all the answers. He wants us to put them on our doorposts so that when we enter our homes we are reminded to LOVE HIM MORE. He wants us to put them on our gates so that when we leave home we are reminded to LOVE HIM MORE.   Let's stop and do a little activity here. Pray before you start to ask God to reveal things to you as you go. Start at your front door, or even outside your front door, and walk from room to room stopping to look at every decoration, every book, and every detail in each room. Ask yourself first is there anything in that room that reminds you to LOVE GOD MORE. Then ask yourself the even harder question, "Is there anything there that you would hide if God came over for a sit-down visit?" Anything that takes our focus off the holiness of God should not be in our homes. Maybe there is a picture with a questionable quote on it. Maybe there is a book or a magazine that should not be there. Maybe you have some clothing in your closet that needs to be removed. Maybe you have some jewelry that needs to be removed. One thing that I stand very strongly opposed to is not allowing peace symbols in my home or in my homeschool group and here is why. The peace symbol came out of the 60s and was created as a symbol to make the statement that religion should be done away with because of its rigid rules. They took a cross and turned it upside down and then broke the cross. I cannot allow that symbol to be in my home because that very cross that it denies, gave me mercy and grace and covers my sin so that I have the opportunity and assurance to spend eternity in heaven with God. I don't care how cute some people might think it is and I don't care how popular it is even among church people. I WILL NOT thumb my nose in God's face and say it is not that big of a deal because the cross is THE DEAL that gives me life. Go through your house and allow God to reveal to you the things that need to be removed and then REMOVE THEM. Now before we leave this section let's cover one more detail – what do you do with the stuff you remove? If you give it away or sell it at a yard sale, are you not aiding someone else to walk away from God? In Acts 19:19-20 we are told of those who practiced magic and they found salvation in Jesus and they burned all their books that were against the teaching of Jesus Christ. Commentaries tell us that the value of the books that they collectively burned was somewhere around $10,000. But verse 20 is what we need to focus on which says, *"So the word of the LORD was growing mightily and prevailing."* Use the Word to tell you what you should do with things that need to be removed from your home and your heart.

Before you turn me off and your defenses build too high for you to overcome let me present an argument to you for you to contemplate for a little while before you continue with this study. I can hear your defenses in your head at this point sounding something like this - "she is just taking all this a little too far." "She is a little too fanatical in all this." "There are plenty of good Christians who have no problem with the peace sign. Even pastor's kids and wives wear things with the peace sign." "Surely God does not expect us to give up everything." "It would be wasteful to just throw away things that I paid good money for." Maybe I hit close to your defense at this point. So here is my argument for you to ponder. Is the society in America better morally and spiritually today than it was 50 years ago? How about 20 years ago? Are we moving as a society closer to God or farther away from God? As all of us know we are snowballing rapidly away from God. If your argument is that even Christian people do it, then that might very well be the reason that we are falling so far away from God. If we do it because everyone else does it, then we will fall headlong into hell with them. If we back up into Acts 5: 12-13, we see that as the disciples were performing many signs and wonders, *"But none of the rest dared to associate with them; however the people held them in high esteem."* It can be lonely serving the Lord in complete obedience to HIS truth. But remember that Jesus taught in Matthew 7 that *"narrow is the gate the leads to life and few are those who find it."* You must decide if you want to follow the crowd through the wide gate that leads to destruction and an eternity in hell or do you want to go with the few through the narrow gate which leads to glory in heaven. You can't choose a little of God and a little of the world. Jesus says that being friends with the world makes you an enemy with God. Your choice is a crucial one, not just for you but for those who follow after you, be that children or friends or onlookers that you may have never even noticed.

Deuteronomy 6:10-19, "Then it shall come about when the Lord your God brings you into the land which He swore to your fathers, Abraham, Isaac and Jacob, to give you, great and splendid cities which you did not build, and houses full of all good things which you did not fill, and hewn cisterns which you did not dig, vineyards and olive trees which you did not plant, and you eat and are satisfied, then watch yourself, that you do not forget the Lord who brought you from the land of Egypt, out of the house of slavery. You shall fear only the Lord your God; and you shall worship Him and swear by His name. You shall not follow other gods, any of the gods of the peoples who surround you, for the Lord your God in the midst of you is a jealous God; otherwise the anger of the Lord your God will be kindled against you, and He will wipe you off the face of the earth. You shall not put the Lord your God to the test, as you tested Him at Massah. You should diligently keep the commandments of the Lord your God, and His testimonies and His statutes which He has commanded you. You shall do what is right and good in the sight of the Lord, that it may be well with you and that you may go in and possess the good land which the Lord swore to give your fathers, by driving out all your enemies from before you, as the Lord has spoken."

When we do the things that God requires of us to do, we will have blessings that we did not get for ourselves and we will have blessings that could only have come from God. You see, what we must realize is this – God loves us so very much that He gave us great detailed instructions of how to live in HIS blessings. He will never make you live in HIS blessings because He didn't want us to be His puppets. He gave us a free will so that we would willingly come to Him and love Him and need Him. How would you feel if your spouse or your children or even your parents came to you every morning and quoted the same exact statement declaring their love for you each day in the exact same manner? It would grow old and cold quickly. But oh how you are moved and touched when someone comes up to you and freely professes his/her love for you. God loves you enough though that He will even put obstacles in front of you to get you to turn back to HIS perfect path that He prepared for you. He wants you, more than you can fathom, to walk in the path that provides His most prefect blessings. The guidelines that He presents to us aren't binding rules that we are punished for if we disobey. That is what Satan wants you to believe. Satan wants us to see God as some great punisher who sits on high and waits for us to mess up so He can slap us on the back of our heads. The exact opposite is true. God stands with the perfect path before us with blessings cascading down the path and He longs for us to walk there. There is life and abundant life and abundant blessings without guilt or shame if we walk in these truths. And IF we do – there will be blessings that we didn't plan or create. There will be an abundance of physical and material needs met in ways that only God could meet. There will be great joy as we walk with Him in obedience receiving HIS perfect blessings. If you "do what is right and good in the sight of the Lord (then) it may be will with you." Determine to drive out the enemies before you – but remember this may be material possessions that need to be driven out of your home and out of your life. It may be those material possessions that are robbing you of your peace.

Deuteronomy 6:20-25, "When your son asks you in time to come, saying, 'What do the testimonies and the statutes and the judgments mean which the Lord our God commanded you?' then you shall say to your son, 'We were slaves to Pharaoh in Egypt, and the Lord brought us from Egypt with a mighty hand. 'Moreover, the Lord showed great and distressing signs and wonders before our eyes against Egypt, Pharaoh and all his household; He brought us out from there in order to bring us in, to give us the land which He had sworn to our fathers.' So the Lord commanded us to observe all these statutes, to fear the Lord our God for our good always and for our survival, as it is today. It will be righteousness for us if we are careful to observe all this commandment before the Lord our God, just as He commanded us."

God put these commandments before us FOR OUR GOOD!! Please don't miss that. They are not there to fence you in, to hold you down and to make you miserable. They are there for your good – for your survival. AND it will be righteousness for you if you are careful to observe all that the Lord commanded you. If you want peace in your life, stop here and determine that God's commandments are for your good. Parents make rules to provide for the safety of their child and they have to issue punishment to train that child to abide within those rules. For instance, a toddler may have a pair of scissors in their hands and decide that it might be interesting to put the tip of those scissors in an electrical outlet. The parent tells the child not to do so but the child tries again. The parent must spank the child or pop them on their hand each time they try to put the tip of the scissors in the outlet to protect the child from harm. It hurts the parents to have to hurt their child BUT they would much prefer the small amount of pain they inflicted for the sake of training their child, rather than have the outcome of letting the child do whatever he wants and die. It is the same with God. He didn't put rules in place to confine us and hurt us. He put rules and guidelines in place to allow us to live a full life and an abundant life. Have a confrontation with Satan and tell him that you will no longer listen to his lies about God being too strict or too hard. Tell him that God's commandments are for your good and that Satan's lies are all meant to harm you and that you will NO LONGER listen to him. Make your stand on the TRUTH of God and put Satan and his lies in their proper place which is out of your life!

*Deuteronomy 11:18-23, "You shall therefore **impress** these words of mine on your heart and on your soul; and you shall **bind them** as a sign on your hand, and they shall be as frontals on your* *forehead. And you shall **teach them** to your sons, **talking of them** when you sit in your house and when you walk along the road and when you lie down and when you rise up. And you shall **write them** on the doorposts of your house and on your gates, so that your days and the days of your sons may be multiplied on the land which the Lord swore to your fathers to give them, as long as the heavens remain above the earth. For **if you are careful to keep** all this commandment which I am commanding you, to do it, to love the Lord your God, to walk in all His ways and hold fast to Him; **then the Lord will** drive out all these nations from before you, and you will dispossess nations greater and mightier than you."*

God reaffirms to the people what He already said but He doesn't want us to miss this. Look at the verbs He uses talking about HIS WORD – impress, bind, teach, talk, write. He doesn't want us to choose one of those – HE wants us to do all of them. Impress – press hard – memorize – bind it to – attach it to – internalize it! He wants HIS Word in me so that no matter if I have a written copy or not – I will forever have His word but so much more than that. You see, when I was a child, I was taught to memorize God's Word so that when I was in trouble or having a bad day I could recall the Scripture and it would make me feel better. This was sooooo very misleading though. I do use God's Word and He recalls it to me in times of stress or in times of ministry to speak into someone else's life. However, God wants HIS Word so deeply imbedded in me that every breath I breathe is filled with Him. Every thought I think is filled with HIS TRUTH. Every action of my every-day, average run-of-the-mill working or relaxing day is filled with HIM. If His word is impressed upon my heart – then I will look at the world differently – through HIS TRUTH every minute of every day. The more of HIS TRUTH I have in me, the more my view changes and THEN I begin to walk in HIS TRUTH and I begin to experience those GOD-sized blessings that HE promises to me. It's my choice. I am not HIS puppet. IF I impress HIS TRUTH in my heart – THEN I will view the world through His eyes – and THEN I will experience the promises of blessings and I will walk in abundant peace.

Let's stop here and take care of another argument before someone reading this dismisses all this based on the lies of the argument. Many people say that the Old Testament is not relevant. Many "self-proclaimed educated" people today claim that it is ancient doctrine that is no longer heeded so why spend time there. Well, my initial comment to that is simply this – if God wanted us to ignore this ancient Jewish law, then He would not have made sure it was included in the Bible that we have today. Then the argument might continue with the fact that it was put there for historical information. Well, I believe, "ALL Scripture is inspired by God and profitable for teaching for reproof, for correction, for training in righteousness; that the man of God may be adequate, equipped for every good work." Paul taught that to Timothy and recorded it in his second letter to Timothy and we find it in the Scripture listed as 2 Timothy 3:16-17.

But that is just me and Paul and what do I know and for that matter what did Paul really know. He was a murderer of Christians before He changed sides. He was just a man who just happened to write the vast majority of the New Testament. You could certainly argue that point. HOWEVER, let's go to Matthew 5:17-18. This is Jesus speaking - and I think He would certainly know what He was talking about. *"Do not think that I came to abolish the Law or the Prophets; I did not come to abolish, but to fulfill. For truly I say to you, 'until heaven and earth pass away, not the smallest letter or stroke shall pass away from the Law, until all is accomplished."*

Jesus showed us another example in Luke 10 about how to apply the laws of the Old Testament to enable us to walk in righteousness and receive the blessings.

Luke 10:25-37 " And a lawyer stood up and put Him to the test, saying, "Teacher, what shall I do to inherit eternal life?" And He said to him, "What is written in the Law? How does it read to you?" And he answered, "YOU SHALL LOVE THE LORD YOUR GOD WITH ALL YOUR HEART, AND WITH ALL YOUR SOUL, AND WITH ALL YOUR STRENGTH, AND WITH ALL YOUR MIND; AND YOUR NEIGHBOR AS YOURSELF." And He said to him, "You have answered correctly; DO THIS AND YOU WILL LIVE." But wishing to justify himself, he said to Jesus, "And who is my neighbor?" Jesus replied and said, "A man was going down from Jerusalem to Jericho, and fell among robbers, and they stripped him and beat him, and went away leaving him half dead. "And by chance a priest was going down on that road, and when he saw him, he passed by on the other side. "Likewise a Levite also, when he came to the place and saw him, passed by on the other side. "But a Samaritan, who was on a journey, came upon him; and when he saw him, he felt compassion, and came to him and bandaged up his wounds, pouring oil and wine on them; and he put him on his own beast, and brought him to an inn and took care of him. "On the next day he took out two denarii and gave them to the innkeeper and said, 'Take care of him; and whatever more you spend, when I return I will repay you.' "Which of these three do you think proved to be a neighbor to the man who fell into the robbers' hands?" And he said, "The one who showed mercy toward him." Then Jesus said to him, "Go and do the same.""

You see Jesus was telling this lawyer, that He was to be true to the TRUTH not the people of his day. God's example showed a priest walking by and going out of his way to ignore the injured man and the Levite, who was from the nation of priests, going to the other side of the road to ignore the needs of the man. Then God used a Samaritan to show as a true neighbor who showed love and care for the injured man. People of that day thought the Samaritans were horrible people. The city of Samaria and the surrounding regions were known for Jews intermarrying with Gentiles and having false gods in their homes. It was mixed marriages and mixed gods for worship. BUT GOD, used a Samaritan as an example of a neighbor. I think Jesus wanted to remind us that it is not our earthly heritage or our social status that makes us worthy or useful to God but the condition of our heart and allowing Him to be LORD. He wants to show the world that we are not judged by our past mistakes but our present condition and our determination to do better. Jesus did not say that we do not have to obey the law as stated in Deuteronomy to love God with everything we have. He explained to us dumb little sheep that we don't obey that law out of heritage or customs, but out of our hearts. He explained that the guidelines set forth in the Old Testament apply to all who call upon the name of the Lord even today. It is for our good and His glory.

So, the first practical thing we have to do is to LOVE God with our whole heart and our whole being. Second, we are going to talk about our brain and our thoughts and what do we do with those thoughts that are the first things that lead us away from God's perfect path.

Phil 4:8-9 "Finally, brethren, whatever is true, whatever is honorable, whatever is right, whatever is pure, whatever is lovely, whatever is of good repute, if there is any excellence and if anything worthy of praise, dwell on these things. The things you have learned and received and heard and seen in me, practice these things, and the God of peace will be with you."

What do you dwell on during the day or during the night? What do you put into your mind? What do you watch on TV or movies? What music do you listen to? What magazines or books do you read? What pages do you 'like' on your social media that posts stuff each day for you to read? What posts do you read from people on your social media? Try this experiment – for a 24 hour period – write down a list of every show you watched on any media source, every movie you watched, every person or group you read from social media, every song you listen to, every magazine you pick up and every person you talk to in person or on the phone or by text. It would be a long list – right? But here is the experiment – beside each one – write down if they were true, honorable, right, pure, lovely, of good repute, excellent, or worthy of praise. If they were not – then why are you allowing them in your mind? You really should add one more category and that would be the commercials you watch in between the movies or shows. You might be watching an uplifting show with a wonderful message but then have to put up with commercials that are far from honorable in any way at all. What we put in our minds, finds its way to our hearts and if allowed to linger there, becomes part of our beliefs and longings.

Let's use a specific example here – many people, many so-called Christian people, have become enamored with the vampire movies. First, if you look up the beginnings of vampires you find that they are from legends of demons that sucked the life-giving blood out of a person. There are many variations of the legends from many different sources but the basic belief from all of them is that the vampire is evil. Well, that then would be detestable to our LORD for us to have any association with them even for our own entertainment. It doesn't matter if it is fiction and we know it is fiction, God's Word tells us to associate with it is detestable to Him and so we would be turning our back on our God and doing what He has clearly said not to do. However, let's say for the sake of argument that you have rationalized that it is OK to go and see these movies. They are very romantic from what I hear about them. You go and you see this actor being this most romantic person that cares for every need and every care of the young maiden. Then you go home. Satan has you right where he wants you. He quickly makes you look closely at your mate. He begins to point out how far from perfect your mate is. He quickly brings someone else in the picture that is more perfect. BUT the one thing he never shows you is how imperfect you are. When we watch these scripted romantic movies, Satan begins to tell us how unsatisfied we are. I have seen this happen in the home of someone very close to me, to the point of divorce being contemplated and it all started with a thought. We must protect what we put in our minds and make sure that we don't give Satan a chance to play with our thoughts. That is why we should filter what we allow in our minds with the verses above from Philippians 4. Remember it was thoughts that led Eve to turn her back on God in a perfect environment. How much more will Satan use that against you in this fallen environment in which we live.

Paul warned Timothy about the fallen environment and just how far we would walk away from God. We need to be aware of this so that we are conscience of everything we allow into our minds.

*2 Tim 3:1-7 "But realize this, that in the last days, difficult times will come. For men will be lovers of self, lovers of money, boastful, arrogant, revilers, disobedient to parents, ungrateful, unholy, unloving, irreconcilable, malicious gossips, without self-control, brutal, haters of good, treacherous, reckless, conceited, **lovers of pleasure rather than lovers of God,** holding to a form of godliness, although they have denied its power; Avoid such men as these. For among them are those who enter into households and captivate weak women weighed down with sins, led on by various impulses, always learning and never able to come to the knowledge of the truth."*

Do we not see this all around us??? We see men and women and boys and girls much more interested in their own pleasure instead of loving God with their whole being. Look at the next phrase after that! "Holding to a form of godliness, although they have denied its power." We see so many people claiming to love God and claiming Jesus as their Savior, but they are unwilling to be obedient to His laws and His ways and through their own denial they have been denied the power that is freely theirs within obedience to God. Again, it is for our good to be obedient. It is for power to grow within us if we obey. The benefits are all ours if we submit to His perfect plan.

What do we also see happening all around us? Look at this next passage.

2 Tim 4:1-5 "I solemnly charge you in the presence of God and of Christ Jesus, who is to judge the living and the dead, and by His appearing and His kingdom: preach the word; be ready in season and out of season; reprove, rebuke, exhort, with great patience and instruction. For the time will come when they will not endure sound doctrine; but wanting to have their ears tickled, they will accumulate for themselves teachers in accordance to their own desires, and will turn away their ears from the truth and will turn aside to myths."

When truth is spoken, people turn away and go and find a 'church' that is willing to tickle the ears of the congregation so that they will be happy and content and be able to continue living in sin and missing the blessings of God. Oh, that my simple words could help you to understand that the pleasures of this world fall eons short of the blessings that are yours in obedience to God.

Before we close this lesson, let's look at some passages about being holy and righteous and living a life of obedience. I want you to read through all the passages below. I will comment intermittently among the passages to keep you focused on the complete thought as we go through them all to obtain the whole counsel of the WORD.

Romans 12:1-2, "I urge you therefore, brethren, by the mercies of God, to present your bodies a living and holy sacrifice, acceptable to God, which is your spiritual service of worship. And do not be conformed to this world, but be transformed by the renewing of your mind, that you may prove what the will of God is, that which is good and acceptable and perfect."

Ephesians 1:3-4, "Blessed by the God and Father of our Lord Jesus Christ, who has blessed us with every spiritual blessing in the heavenly places in Christ, just as He chose us in Him before the foundation of the world, that we should be holy and blameless before Him."

*2 Corinthians 6:14-7:1, "Do not be bound together with unbelievers; for what partnership have righteousness and lawlessness, or what fellowship has light with darkness? Or what harmony has Christ with Belial, or what has a believer in common with an unbeliever? Or what agreement has the temple of God with idols? For we are the temple of the living God; just as God said, 'I will dwell in them and walk among them; and I will be their God, and they shall be My people. Therefore **come out** from their midst and be separate,' says the Lord. 'And do not touch what is unclean; and I will welcome you. And I will be a father to you, and you shall be sons and daughters to Me.' Says the Lord Almighty. Therefore, having these promises, beloved, let us cleanse ourselves from all defilement of flesh and spirit, perfecting holiness in the fear of God."*

WE ARE TO BE HOLY AND RIGHTEOUS AND OBEDIENT TO GOD. BUT – it is sooooo hard – right???

Col 1:19-23 "For it was the Father's good pleasure for all the fullness to dwell in Him, and through Him to reconcile all things to Himself, having made peace through the blood of His cross; through Him, I say, whether things on earth or things in heaven. And although you were formerly alienated and hostile in mind, engaged in evil deeds, yet He has now reconciled you in His fleshly body through death, in order to present you before Him holy and blameless and beyond reproach — if indeed you continue in the faith firmly established and steadfast, and not moved away from the hope of the gospel that you have heard, which was proclaimed in all creation under heaven, and of which I, Paul, was made a minister."

Isaiah 6:5-7, "Then I said, 'Woe is me, for I am ruined! Because I am a man of unclean lips, and I live among a people of unclean lips; for my eyes have seen the King, the Lord of hosts.' Then one of the seraphim flew to me, with a burning coal in his hand which he had taken from the altar with tongs. And he touched my mouth with it and said, 'Behold, this has touched your lips; and your iniquity is taken away and your sin is forgiven."

You see, we can't be perfectly holy. Only through the blood of Jesus and the touch of God can our sins be forgiven and we be deemed holy and perfect and righteous. If we could perfect ourselves, then there would have been NO need for Jesus to be our sacrifice. Keep reading and don't give up because there is such great hope here if you follow through to the end.

Ps 24:1-5, "The earth is the Lord's, and all it contains, The world, and those who dwell in it. For He has founded it upon the seas And established it upon the rivers. Who may ascend into the hill of the Lord? And who may stand in His holy place? He who has clean hands and a pure heart, Who has not lifted up his soul to falsehood And has not sworn deceitfully. He shall receive a blessing from the Lord And righteousness from the God of his salvation."

1 John 2:4-6, "The one who says, " I have come to know Him," and does not keep His commandments, is a liar, and the truth is not in him; but whoever keeps His word, in him the love of God has truly been perfected. By this we know that we are in Him: the one who says he abides in Him ought himself to walk in the same manner as He walked."

1 John 2:15-17, "Do not love the world nor the things in the world. If anyone loves the world, the love of the Father is not in him. For all that is in the world, the lust of the flesh and the lust of the eyes and the boastful pride of life, is not from the Father, but is from the world. The world is passing away, and also its lusts; but the one who does the will of God lives forever."

SO – how do we reconcile all these verses about holiness and grace?

Paul wrote so eloquently in Romans 6 about this very thing.

Romans 6, "What shall we say then? Are we to continue in sin so that grace may increase? May it never be! How shall we who died to sin still live in it? Or do you not know that all of us who have been baptized into Christ Jesus have been baptized into His death? Therefore, we have been buried with Him through baptism into death, so that as Christ was raised from the dead through the glory of the Father, so we too might walk in newness of life. For if we have become united with Him in the likeness of His death, certainly we shall also be in the likeness of His resurrection, knowing this, that our old self was crucified with Him, in order that our body of sin might be done away with, so that we would no longer be slaves to sin; for he who has died is freed from sin. Now if we have died with Christ, we believe that we shall also live with Him, knowing that Christ, having been raised from the dead, is never to die again; death no longer is master over Him. For the death that He died, He died to sin once for all; but the life that He lives, He lives to God. Even so consider yourselves to be dead to sin, but alive to God in Christ Jesus. Therefore do not let sin reign in your mortal body so that you obey its lusts, and do not go on presenting the members of your body to sin as instruments of unrighteousness; but present yourselves to God as those alive from the dead, and your members as instruments of righteousness to God. For sin shall not be master over you, for you are not under law but under grace. What then? Shall we sin because we are not under law but under grace? May it never be! Do you not know that when you present yourselves to someone as slaves for obedience, you are slaves of the one whom you obey, either of sin resulting in death, or of obedience resulting in righteousness? But thanks be to God that though you were slaves of sin, you became **_obedient from the heart to that form of teaching to which you were committed_**, and having been freed from sin, you became slaves of righteousness. I am speaking in human terms because of the weakness of your flesh. For just as you presented your members as slaves to impurity and to lawlessness, resulting in further lawlessness, so now present your members as slaves to righteousness, resulting in sanctification. For when you were slaves *of sin, you were free in regard to righteousness. Therefore what benefit were you then deriving from the things of which you are now ashamed? For the outcome of those things is death. But now having been freed from sin and enslaved to God, you derive your benefit, resulting in sanctification, and the outcome, eternal life. For the wages of sin is death, but the free gift of God is eternal life in Christ Jesus our Lord."*

For you see, Paul is trying to tell us that we are to be slaves to righteousness. We are going to sin but we don't have to live in that sin. We need to recognize it and walk toward holiness. We need to be obedient from the heart to God's teachings. Then and only then, will we be able to not only find peace but live in peace no matter what our current circumstances are. May God our heavenly Father, lead and guide you into obedience and shower you with abundant blessings and peace that only He can give. Walk out your life in obedience and you will walk through your life in unshakeable peace. There will still be plenty of trials and tribulations and many dark valleys, BUT God will walk through them with you covering you with His perfect peace.

ABOUT THE AUTHOR

Julia Wright Fortenberry is a wife of 38 years, a mother, a grandmother, and teacher. She received her National Teaching Certification while teaching in public school. From that experience, God called her to be one of the founders of a Christian school in her local church where she served as teacher and administrator for 10 years. She is co-founder with her daughter, Jennifer Browder, of Truth Learning Center, which is a homeschool group located on her family farm. The students help on the farm as it is being rebuilt after many years of neglect. Julia leads her students to participate in widow ministries to not only teach them biblical ministry but through that ministry to teach them compassion for elders, training them that our elders are not disposable at any age or physical health condition. Another way she trains her high school students, and many times their parents, is in being willing to stop and pray with and minister to those who stop by during the day, teaching them that we can never be too busy to minister in the name of Jesus.

She has taught Bible classes for all ages from preschool through adults. Just before her 50th birthday God led her into a deeper study of His Word and she began writing Bible lessons for His glory. Julia was moved by the Holy Spirit to write in everyday language the TRUTH of the Bible and not depend upon religious doctrine to teach her TRUTH. She writes daily Facebook devotions and authors **www.bountifulblessings2017.wordpress.com**. She has a heart for God's Word and a calling to share it as absolute TRUTH but in everyday language that everyone can relate to.